Let's Crochet!

Kalmbach Books
21027 Crossroads Circle
Waukesha, Wisconsin 53186
www.Kalmbach.com/books

Published in 2009
13 12 11 10 09 1 2 3 4 5

Manufactured in the United States of America

ISBN: 978-0-87116-272-4

Publisher's Cataloging-in-Publication Data
Satterfield, Monette Lassiter.
  Let's crochet! : the beginner's guide to crocheting / by Monette Satterfield.

  p. : ill. ; cm.

  ISBN: 978-0-87116-272-4

1. Crocheting–Technique. 2. Crocheting–Patterns. I. Title.

TT820 .S288 2009
746.434

The **beginner's guide** to crocheting

Let's Crochet!

by Monette Satterfield

KALMBACH BOOKS

Contents

6 WHY LEARN TO CROCHET?

GETTING STARTED

8 MATERIALS & TOOLS

9 Yarn

11 Patterns

13 Gauge

14 Tools and Equipment

16 HOW TO CROCHET

16 Holding the Hook and Yarn

17 Basic Stitches

25 Finishing

27 Embellishments

93 CARE OF FINISHED PROJECTS

94 RESOURCES

95 Acknowledgments and About the Author

PROJECTS

WEARABLES

30 Simply Soft Scarf

33 Chic Kerchief

36 Classic Neck & Wrist Warmers

39 Beautiful Brimmed Hat

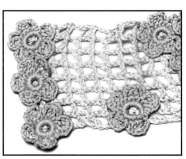

43 Feminine Floral Scarf

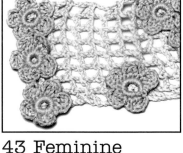

46 Strappy Cami

49 Lacy Wrap Overskirt

52 Wrap Around Shawl

FOR THE HOME

56 Shaped
Market Bag

59 Casual
Cushion

62 Not Your
Granny's Rug

65 Get Organized
Storage Baskets

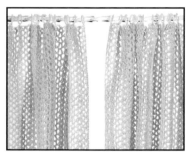

68 Lacy Café
Curtains

71 Table Runner &
Place Mats

74 Felted Basket

GREAT GIFTS

78 Kitty Cushion
& Toy

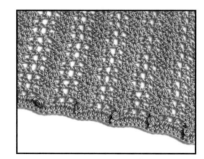

81 Beginner Baby
Blanket

84 Cute Crochet
Critters

87 Felted Oven
Mitts

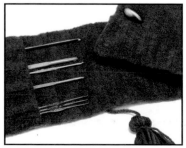

90 Felted
Hook Book

Why Learn to Crochet?

There are so many reasons to learn to crochet! Many people crochet for pure enjoyment. They love the materials and find the rhythmic quality of the work soothing and meditative. Others enjoy crocheting in groups and workshops, learning and sharing experiences in conferences, blogs, and forums. This sense of community is strong, and it can be a compelling reason to join in.

To me, the most compelling reason to crochet, or to want to learn to crochet, is to celebrate being able to create something yourself. More and more people seem to just know *about* something rather than how to do it. Being able to crochet is about valuing well-made and beautiful things and not just having them.

On a Personal Note

I learned to crochet when I was 12 years old from a how-to booklet with some help from my mother. Quite a few of my family members crocheted, and they usually worked with acrylic yarn making afghans. I was fascinated by thread crochet and made a number of doilies and other items that I still have.

After several years of making fine thread crochet items, crochet fell into the background due to other interests and a lack of appealing patterns. When I did pick it up again, I was newly married and setting up my first home. There weren't many attractive and useful patterns, so I discovered the key to designing my own projects: gauge and simple math. Having learned the magic of crochet design, I started designing my own projects. My first design was a two-color, single-crochet pillow cover. From there, the projects gradually progressed in complexity. During this time, I was fortunate enough to own the local yarn store, where I learned how to teach the basics and find and fix problems in someone else's work.

HOW TO USE THIS BOOK

The patterns in this book are for beginners and are easy, fun, and can be customized. Many of them are great gifts for those same reasons.

All crochet, no matter how fancy, is based on the same set of stitches and skills. Once you learn the first skills involved in making chain and single crochet stitches, the techniques build from there. Crochet is a flexible craft. There are no strict rules, just guidelines. There are no crochet police!

A note about the yarns used in this book: Despite their popularity, the fuzzy, furry, and fluffy novelty yarns are not used here. They are more difficult for a beginner to work with and make the stitches hard to see. While you are learning the basics, you need to be able to see the stitches. Smooth yarns help you do that.

The best way to learn to crochet is just to get started. If you already know how to chain and work basic crochet stitches, pick any project that appeals to you. The scarf, table runner, and casual cushion are great projects for learning the basics. Once you get going on a project, refer to the basics section on pages 16–28 if you need a little help. Also don't be afraid to ask someone who crochets. Needleworkers are very helpful, so just ask!

You can also learn crochet techniques from books. Consider building your own personal reference library. It will come in handy as your skills develop and you take on more challenging projects. Different authors also have different ways of writing instructions, which can help you understand a new technique better. Some suggestions to get you started are listed in the references section.

Learning Style

We don't all learn the same way. I like to read instructions, then try it myself. Some people prefer to be shown how to do something, and others prefer verbal explanations. Don't hesitate to try something different if the method you're using is not working.

Crochet is one of the few forms of needlework that cannot be produced by machine. This makes it an ideal medium for personal expression. You will be able to create a garment or home décor item that cannot be found in any store. After all, anyone can buy something, but not everyone can make it.

Learning to crochet is much more than just being able to make the stitches. It's about gaining confidence in yourself and your abilities. Of course, there are mistakes to be made—I've made plenty

Creative Options

At the end of the project instructions is a section called "Creative Options." These are suggestions to make the pattern a little bit different from the written instructions. There are many ways to customize a pattern and make it your own—these are just a starting point.

The techniques used in the pattern are listed for each project. Check to see what techniques are required, and read through the pattern. If you're unsure of something, look it up and then proceed with confidence.

myself—but you can make mistakes and then go on to produce beautiful things. I hope you will approach the whole undertaking with a spirit of adventure. It's just yarn, after all!

Getting Started

Materials & Tools

YARN

I love yarn in all its forms! There are many types and qualities of yarn available today. The yarns in this book were especially selected to showcase a wide range of types and brands. Quality is available at most price levels.

Fibers

Fiber refers to the type of material yarns are made from. They fall into two basic categories: natural and synthetic. Natural fibers include animal fibers, such as wool, mohair, alpaca, cashmere, and silk, and vegetable fibers such as cotton, linen, and ramie.

Fiber Types

- **Wool** is easy to work with, comfortable to wear, and a great fiber to use while learning to crochet. Wool is spun from sheep fleece, and it is available in many types and quality levels. Wool is warm, elastic, durable, and easy to dye. It also insulates and absorbs water well.
- **Mohair** is an extremely lightweight and warm fiber made from goat fleece.

Yarn Structure

Spinning is the basic method of making yarn from raw fibers. Strands of yarn are composed of fibers twisted together. Each strand of fiber is known as a **ply**, and the yarn is made up of a number of plies spun together. The number of plies has little to do with the weight of the yarn, but it can affect how much loft the yarn has. **Loft** is the amount of air trapped inside a yarn between the fibers themselves and the strands that form the yarn. Garments made of high-loft yarn are warm and hold their shape.

Four strands of fiber make up this 4-ply yarn.

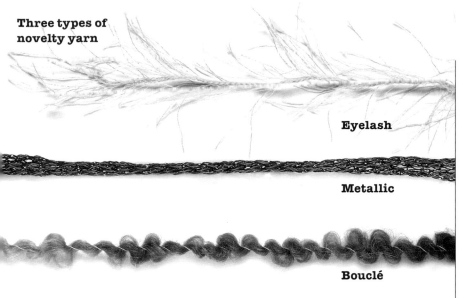

Three types of novelty yarn

Eyelash

Metallic

Bouclé

- **Alpaca** yarns are made from the shorn coat of the alpaca.
- **Angora** comes from the soft fur of Angora rabbits. It is very warm, soft, and silky, but it can be inelastic.
- **Cashmere** fibers are from the cashmere goat. Due to the tedious collection process, cashmere can be expensive.
- **Silk** is made from the filaments of the silkworm cocoon. The fiber is strong but not elastic.
- **Cotton** fibers come from the seed pod, or boll, of the cotton plant. It is absorbent, but yarns made entirely of cotton can be heavy and inelastic.
- **Linen** fibers are derived from the stems of the flax plant. Like cotton, linen is very absorbent but lacks resilience. Linen is usually blended with other fibers to produce yarn.
- **Rayon** is made of naturally occurring cellulose material that is formed into fibers.
- **Bamboo** is a soft, comfortable, lustrous fiber that is often blended with other fibers.
- **Synthetic** fibers are easy to clean, durable, and inexpensive. Blends of synthetic and natural fibers can produce practical, beautiful yarn. Common synthetic fibers include nylon, acrylic, polyester, and rayon.

Weight

Yarn is categorized by weight. This is not how much a ball of yarn actually weighs; it refers to a classification system that divides yarns into categories based on how thick or thin they are. Each weight category corresponds to a particular range of stitch gauges and needle sizes.

The confusing part is that different countries, or even needleworkers, may have different terms for the same yarn weight. The table below shows some terms used to refer to yarn weights and the average number of stockinette (knit) stitches or single crochet stitches over 4 in. (10cm).

When choosing a pattern, pay attention to the yarn weight specified. Using a thicker yarn makes a project go quickly because there are fewer stitches per inch and row. Thicker yarns often produce a warmer fabric than thinner yarns because of loft (see "Yarn Structure"). Using a thick yarn with a high loft produces a hefty, bulky fabric. A thinner yarn may not have the insulating loft of a bulky yarn, but it will result in a light, manageable fabric.

Weight	Type	Crochet Gauge	Knit Gauge	YS Symbol
Superfine	Sock	21–32 stitches	27–32 stitches	**1** SUPER FINE
	Fingering			
	Baby			
Fine	Sport	16–20 stitches	23–26 stitches	**2** FINE
	Baby			
Light	DK	12–17 stitches	21–24 stitches	**3** LIGHT
	Light Worsted			
Medium	Worsted	11–14 stitches	16–20 stitches	**4** MEDIUM
	Afghan			
	Aran			
Bulky	Chunky	8–11 stitches	12–15 stitches	**5** BULKY
	Craft			
	Rug			
Super Bulky	Bulky	5–9 stitches	6–11 stitches	**6** SUPER BULKY
	Roving			

Source: Craft Yarn Council of America, www.yarnstandards.com

When choosing a yarn, you should also consider ply, or strand, which refers to the number of threads that have been twisted together to create the yarn. You can count the number of plies in most yarns by untwisting the end. Some novelty yarns consist of just one strand. The weight of the plied yarn is not related to the number of strands; it refers to the thickness of the individual strands.

Colors and Dye Lots

Most yarn is dyed in batches or dye lots, which can vary slightly from one to another. Be sure to buy enough yarn from the same dye lot to finish your project. Even if it looks the same in the ball, it often will show a slight difference when worked into a garment. Besides, having extra yarn enhances your stash.

An exciting development in the world of yarn is specialty dyed yarn. You can choose from luscious hand-dyed hanks from small companies to lovely machine-dyed yarns that make complicated patterns as you work.

TIP: *Stash* is a word used in yarn terminology. It refers to yarn waiting to be made into projects or, more likely, yarn purchased without a specific project in mind.

Ball, Skein, or Hank?

Yarn is available in balls, skeins, and hanks. Balls are what they sound like: yarn wound into a shape resembling a ball. Yarn is worked from the outside of the ball. Skeins are bundles of yarn, some of which are designed as pull skeins. These often have an end sticking out to so you can work from the center. Hanks are loose circles of yarn twisted up

Yarn is available in balls, skeins and hanks.

hank

skein

ball

into a little package. To work with hanks, you will have to wind the yarn into a ball.

There are a few different ways to turn a tangle-prone loop of yarn into a tidy ball. You can use a ball winder and a swift, a gadget that holds the skein and feeds the yarn to the winder so all you have to do is turn the handle. You can also arrange the hank around the back of one or two straight chairs and wind the ball by hand, or have a helper hold the hank looped over their arms while you wind the ball by hand. (Just be sure that your helper's arms don't get too tired!)

Quantities

The quantities listed for the projects are accurate, but you may find that you need more or less yarn for a specific project. Any changes to the pattern may change the amount of yarn needed. If the sample project shown used up the entire amount of yarn, that is noted in the pattern, and you may want to purchase more yarn to be sure you have enough.

Choosing a Yarn

Quality yarn is well-spun, has good color, and feels good. For example, the wool isn't grainy and

scratchy, and the acrylic doesn't feel like plastic. Quality yarn also passes an in-store durability test: Rub a strand firmly between two fingers and check for loose fibers and unusual breakdown of the strand. If you are sensitive to certain fibers, check the labels and rub the ball or skein vigorously on the inside of your forearm. Any redness or irritation is a warning not to use this fiber next to your skin.

You may hear the term *yarn snob*, which refers to a person who only buys and uses exclusive, expensive yarn. That's not me! I think there are good qualities in almost all yarn. If you like the yarn and the item you made from it, it is a perfect yarn!

Where to Buy Yarn

You can shop craft and hobby stores, the local yarn store, and even online. Buying in person allows you to touch the yarn and evaluate the quality of your purchase, but you are limited to the store's selection. Online buying opens up many possibilities, but it also keeps you from the all-important touch-and-feel experience.

PATTERNS

One of the best things about making things for yourself is that you are in complete control of the item you make. You choose the yarn, the color, the fit, and the finishing details.

To help you make those choices, there are some things to consider that will make the process easier. Think about color: Which colors are most flattering on you? Don't get caught up in bargain fever—there's a reason 15 balls of merino wool in that unusual color are on sale. Don't fall for it!

Next, consider what it is about similar items you have that you like and dislike. If you don't like oversized shapes, you will not wear a large lace topper. The same goes for more subtle details, like a crewneck instead of a v-neck or a cardigan instead of a pullover.

Finally, note your fiber preferences. You may prefer cotton and blends to wool. Your climate may not be suitable for wool. If you are indoors most of the time, you may not have a need for a bulky wool sweater, no matter how much fun it might be to make.

Fit

Garment instructions are usually given in a range of sizes. These sizes are often expressed as a measurement in inches or centimeters, or as S, M, L, etc. Be sure to compare your actual measurement to the listed size to ensure the item will fit properly. Even if you normally wear a size medium, you will find that the finished item will be larger by some amount. This is the wearing and design ease built into the pattern by the designer, and it can range from a slightly negative amount (which would be a skin-

ABBREVIATIONS

Here is a list of common abbreviations in crochet patterns. Not all these abbreviations have been used in the patterns in this book.

( ): work instructions within parentheses as directed
* *: repeat instructions between asterisks as directed
*: repeat the instructions following the single asterisk as directed
[ ]: work instructions within brackets as directed
alt: alternate
approx: approximately
beg: begin/beginning
bet: between
BL: back loop(s),
bo: bobble
BP: back post
BPdc: back-post double crochet
BPsc: back-post single crochet
BPtr: back-post treble crochet
CA: color A
CB: color B
CC: contrasting color
ch: chain stitch
ch-sp: chain space
CL: cluster
cm: centimeter(s)
cont: continue
dc: double crochet
dc2tog: double crochet two stitches together
dec: decrease/decreases/decreasing
dtr: double treble,
FL: front loop(s)
foll: follow/follows/following
FP: front post
FPdc: front post double

crochet
FPsc: front post single crochet
FPtr: front post treble crochet
g: gram
hdc: half-double crochet
inc: increase/increases/increasing
lp(s): loops
m: meter(s)
MC: main color
mm: millimeter(s)
oz: ounce(s)
p: picot
pat(s) or patt: pattern(s)
pc: popcorn
pm: place marker
prev: previous
rem: remain/remaining
rep: repeat(s)
rnd(s): round(s)
RS: right side
sc: single crochet
sc2tog: single crochet 2 stitches together
sk: skip
sl st: slip sitch
sp(s): space(s)
st(s): stitch(es)
tbl: through back loop
tch or t-ch: turning chain
tog: together
tr: treble crochet
trtr: triple treble crochet
WS: wrong side
yd: yard(s)
yo: yarn over

tight garment) to as much as 8 in. (20cm) more than the body inside.

Compare your measurements to the finished size listed in the pattern and consider the amount of ease allowed. For a comparison,

standard fitting garments allow approximately 4 in. (10cm) of ease. Don't be tempted to drastically reduce or eliminate the ease, or your garment may not fit properly.

Reading the Pattern

At first, the pattern may look as if it were written in some other language. But don't worry; there is logic to it. The abbreviations are usually standard, and they are listed in the pattern with the steps presented in a systematic manner.

First, sit down and read the pattern through when you are not in a rush or distracted. This will allow you to check any unfamiliar abbreviations and see how the piece is put together. If there are multiple sizes, mark the size you need throughout the pattern to avoid confusion later. Look up and practice any techniques with which you're unfamiliar.

The punctuation in patterns helps you move through a row or set of stitches. Particular patterns may vary, but there are similarities between patterns.

Periods usually mean the end of a row. Commas and semicolons are used mid-row to set off specific instructions or series of instructions. Parentheses can indicate multiple sizes or the repetition of a sequence of stitches. Asterisks may also be used for the same purpose, and they may refer you to an earlier portion of the instructions to avoid repeating it.

TIP: Keep an eye out for parentheses for multiple sizes and mark them for clarity if necessary.

Pattern Stitch Diagrams

Stitch diagrams for pattern stitches have been included with the projects in this book. Working from diagrams instead of written instructions is also referred to as symbol crochet. If you have never used stitch diagrams, you may be surprised at how much of a

difference they can make. Give them a try and see if they are helpful for you.

Think of the diagrams as "maps" of the crochet fabric. The symbols used approximate the look of the actual stitches they represent. The diagrams show you what you are going to do before you start, and they help you keep track of your position in the work. To use diagrams, familiarize yourself with the basic stitches and the symbols that represent them. For example, from double-crochet onward, the number of short, angled strokes crossing the stem of a symbol represents the number of times the yarn is wrapped before the hook is inserted.

Read diagrams in the direction the crochet is worked. Allover patterns are worked from the bottom to the top, and individual elements (or motifs, such as flowers) are worked from the center outward.

Stitch Patterns

Stitch patterns are based on repeats of stitches and rows. The stitch sequence repeats across a row, and a series of rows of those stitch sequences repeats vertically. Together they make up a stitch pattern that determines how your crocheted fabric will look. The individual stitch pattern instructions explain how to make the stitches and rows that make up a single repeat.

Stitch pattern instructions sometimes begin by giving you a

multiple of starting chain stitches (the foundation of crochet—see p. 17) that make a complete repeat of the pattern. Sometimes you have to crochet an extra chain stitch or two to make a specific pattern work out. When you make a swatch, make a multiple of the number of chains called for plus the extra chain(s). For example, if the pattern calls for a multiple of 2 chains plus 3, you could chain 13 (2 x 5 + 3), or 9 (2 x 3 + 3), or some other such calculation.

Common crochet symbols

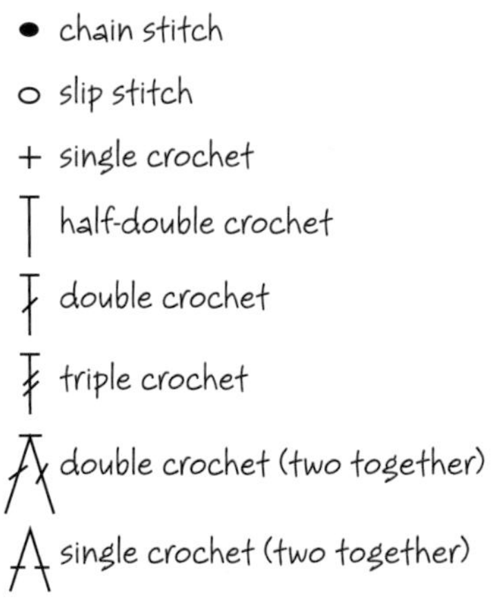

- ● chain stitch
- ○ slip stitch
- + single crochet
- ⊤ half-double crochet
- �f double crochet
- ⨍ triple crochet
- ⋏ double crochet (two together)
- ⋀ single crochet (two together)

Flower motif example

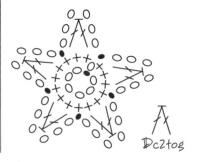

Dc2tog

GAUGE

Achieving the correct gauge is the key to making pieces the correct size. Gauge is the number of stitches and rows per inch, including fractions of stitches. This information is crucial to the success of any item that must fit properly or be the correct size when finished. Most patterns include a recommended gauge. The patterns in this book include directions for making the gauge swatch. For some projects, such as scarves and blankets, the exact gauge is not important, and that is noted as well.

Gauge depends on many things: the yarn, the size of the tools used, the pattern stitch used, and most especially, you. The gauge you obtain is uniquely yours, since everyone holds the hook with a different amount of tension to make stitches.

The gauge can also vary among different colors of the same yarn—black yarn can work much differently than lighter colors. Because different colored yarns can react differently, you may want to make a gauge swatch with each color if you are using multiple colors in a project.

Gauge can also be influenced by the type of hook you use. You may obtain a different gauge using aluminum tools than you would with wood or plastic. Crochet hooks can vary significantly in size and style, and this variation affects the gauge as well. Gauge is affected by yarn substitutions, too.

No matter what the pattern and yarn label say, check your gauge for every project with the hook you are going to use, even if you have used that same yarn before. A different gauge will result in a larger or smaller finished item. You can still substitute yarns, but be sure to work a gauge swatch and adjust your hook size if needed.

Make a Gauge Swatch

Unless otherwise directed by the pattern, crochet a 6-in. (15cm) square in the stitch specified, using the hook size noted in the pattern. While a 6-in. (15cm) square is adequate for measuring gauge in most cases, a larger swatch may be better. The thicker the yarn, the bigger the swatch should be. If the pattern stitch has a repeat of a certain number of stitches, make the swatch large enough to accommodate at least one repeat. If you plan to launder your finished item, wash the swatch in the same manner. Likewise, if blocking the project pieces, block the swatch.

Lay the swatch flat, and place two pins 4 in. (10cm) apart horizontally and vertically. Be sure to lay the swatch on a firm surface. Count the number of stitches and rows between the pins. Be sure to count fractions of stitches if they exist. They can make a significant difference in the finished item. If your gauge does not match the pattern's gauge, don't stretch or compress the swatch to make it conform to the pattern. If you have fewer stitches than the pattern requires, switch to a smaller hook and work another gauge swatch. If your work has more stitches than required, try using a larger hook.

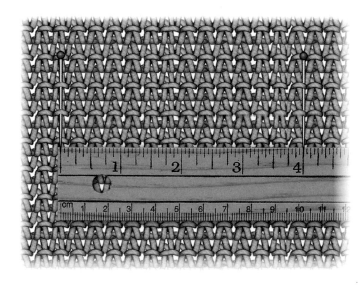

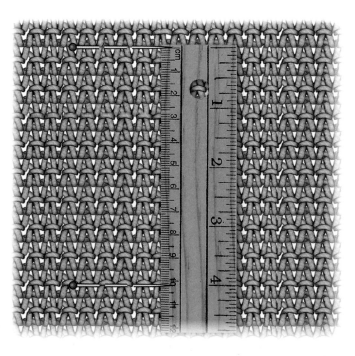

TOOLS AND EQUIPMENT
Hooks

All you need to crochet is a hook and some yarn. Hooks are made of metal, plastic, wood, resin, and bamboo. The sizes range from tiny steel hooks small enough to use with thread to large plastic hooks for the bulkiest yarns. A standard hook is about 6 in. (15cm) long.

There are different sizing systems for crochet hooks, including a metric size; the U.S. sizing system, which uses letters and numbers; and the U.K./Canadian system. Steel hooks for thread crochet have a separate numbering system, from U.S. size 14 (0.75mm), the smallest, to U.S. size E/4 (3.5mm). This book uses the U.S. system in addition to metric sizes.

CROCHET HOOK SIZES

Millimeter	U.S. Size
2.25 mm	B/1
2.75mm	C/2
3.25mm	D/3
3.5mm	E/4
3.75mm	F/5
4mm	G/6
4.5mm	7
5mm	H/8
5.5mm	I/9
6mm	J/10
6.5mm	K/10½
8mm	L/11
9mm	M–N/13
10mm	N–P/15
15mm	P–Q
16mm	Q
19mm	S

Source: Craft Yarn Council of America, www.YarnStandards.com

About the Hook

A crochet hook has four distinct parts that affect the work.

The **point** is inserted into the stitches of the crocheted fabric. A too-round point may be hard to insert and a too-sharp point can split the yarn.

The **throat** catches the yarn to bring it back through the loops and stitches. It must be large enough to hold the yarn being used. The shape of the throat can vary significantly among hooks.

The **shank** holds loops while working, and it is the part of the hook that determines the size of the stitches and gauge. Be sure to insert the hook fully into the work and loops for accuracy.

The **thumb rest** is a flattened spot for resting your thumb or other fingers. It makes grasping and maneuvering the hook much easier.

These four parts vary among brands, so try several different types of hooks to determine which type you prefer. All this variability makes it even more important that you test the gauge for a project, because even two hooks labeled the same size can yield different gauges. If you are having trouble catching the yarn to pull it through, or if the yarn splits frequently, try a different hook. One type of hook has a slightly rounded point and tapered throat, and the other (called an inline hook) has a sharper point and a wider throat.

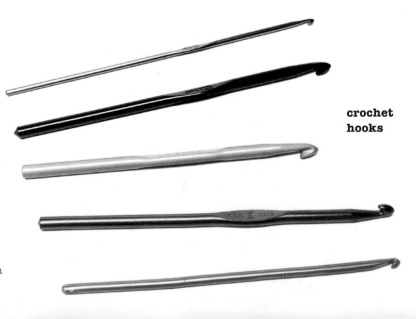

crochet hooks

Accessories

Even though a hook and yarn are all you really need to start crocheting, there are many accessories that can make it easier.

- **Tape measure:** Buy a good-quality tape measure and replace it occasionally, as it can stretch and become inaccurate.
- **Stitch and hook gauge:** This is very helpful for measuring swatches and sizing hooks. Slide the shank of your hook into the smallest hole that fits, and read the corresponding number to determine the size of your hook.
- **Stitch marker rings:** Avoid the round markers used on knitting needles. Use split rings or markers that can be opened to hang onto the work to mark stitches and rows.
- **Safety pins:** An old standby, safety pins have many uses. Try to find coil-less pins to keep from snagging your yarn.
- **Yarn needles:** These needles have large eyes and blunt tips for weaving in ends, sewing up seams, and attaching buttons or trims.
- **Scissors:** Buy a small, sharp pair for cutting yarn.
- **Plastic head pins or T-pins:** Pins with large plastic heads help hold thick pieces together. Pins with large heads are clearly visible in the work.
- **Storage bags:** These can range from a zippered bag to a designer tote.
- **Other accessories:** There are plenty of other items you may need or want. Browse the accessory department of your local store or look online for the latest can't-do-without gadgets!

For Beginners

If you are just starting, you don't need every single accessory—a basic set of tools will cover most situations. You will need:

- A small, sharp pair of scissors for cutting yarn and thread
- A good-quality measuring tape
- Stitch markers and safety pins in different sizes
- Yarn or tapestry needles
- Long, heavy pins with plastic heads for pinning pieces together.

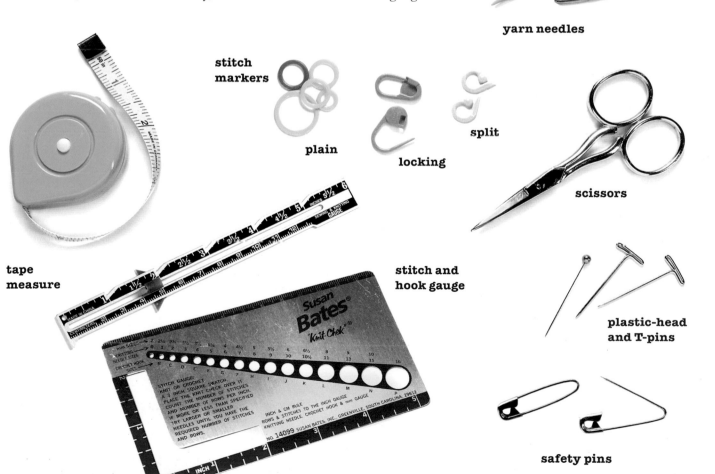

yarn needles

stitch markers

plain

locking

split

scissors

tape measure

stitch and hook gauge

plastic-head and T-pins

safety pins

Getting Started

How to Crochet

HOLDING THE HOOK AND YARN

How you hold the crochet hook is your choice. Use whatever method is comfortable and works for you. The two most common methods of holding a crochet hook are shown here. Do not grip the hook tightly, and keep your wrist straight to minimize strain on your hands.

Holding the yarn properly allows you to maintain control and tension of the yarn as it flows through your fingers. Good, even tension is neither too tight nor too loose. The yarn should be taut enough to easily catch it with the hook but loose enough to allow you to pull it and the hook through the stitches.

Hold the hook in your dominant hand, and wrap the working yarn around the fingers of your non-dominant hand. Your non-dominant hand will control the yarn from the ball, and you will use the section of yarn that runs between the hook and your index finger. Your index finger will move up and down as you work to create an even tension.

There are various ways to hold and keep tension on the yarn. For options, see the illustration on the next page. Experiment with different ways to work with the yarn and find a method that is comfortable. Keep practicing, and don't worry if it feels terribly awkward at first. For left-handed instructions, see p. 24.

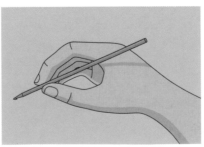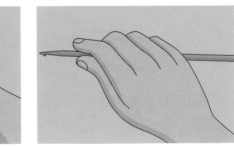

Holding the crochet hook

Make a Slip Knot

A crocheter begins by placing a slip knot on the hook. Then, another loop is pulled through the first. This is repeated to form a chain, which begins almost every crochet project. Then, loops are pulled up to form the basic stitches. The slip knot secures the yarn to the hook and is not counted as a stitch.

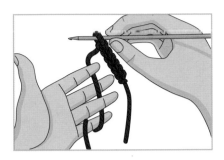

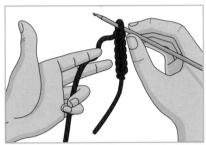

The left hand is shown palm-up to illustrate the path of the yarn. When working, both of your hands will be palm down.

- Begin by crossing the end of the yarn under the main length of yarn from the ball to make a loop. Place the yarn coming from the ball (the working yarn) above the loop. Insert your hook as shown above.

- Hold onto the loose yarn tail with your pinkie or index finger to keep it from slipping. Hook the working yarn (from the ball) with the hook and pull it through the loop from back to front.

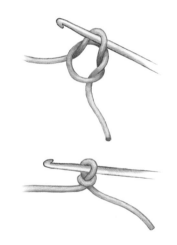

- Pull the working yarn gently to tighten the slip knot around the hook.

TIP: Be sure to leave a tail of yarn at least 6-in. (15cm) long for working in easily.

BASIC STITCHES

Crochet stitches are formed by a series of loops made around the hook and pulled through other loops. Every stitch pattern, no matter how complex, is made up of the same basic stitches, which are made up of these loops. All the stitches are made using a similar set of movements. The stitches are presented here in general order of height and number of loops.

Chain Stitch (ch)

Nearly every crochet project starts with chain stitches as a base. Chain stitches are used to create openings in the work for lace patterns and as turning chains to add height at the start of a new row or round. These first chain stitches are sometimes called the foundation chain, and they form the beginning edge of your project.
- Begin with a slip knot.
- Wrap the yarn around the hook from back to front and pull it through the loop, holding onto the slip knot. Pull lightly to tighten. Repeat to make a row of chain stitches.

Practice Makes Perfect

To practice, choose a smooth worsted-weight wool yarn and a size H/8 (5mm) or I/9 (5.5mm) hook. Wool is pliable, easy to work with, and forgiving. Start with an easy project, like the "Simply Soft Scarf," p. 30. You'll learn to use your new skills and have a great accessory when you're done.

Work chain stitches at the thickest part of the hook shank (see "About the Hook," p. 14) to keep them from being too tight. A too-tight starting chain is a common problem. If your starting chain is too tight, try using a hook one or two sizes larger. It's very important to make adjustments for the tightness or looseness of the foundation chain while working the sample swatch. The extra bit of effort can save a lot of time ripping out and reworking later.

Counting chain stitches accurately is important, as many projects start with a long chain. Make sure the front of the foundation chain is facing you. The front has a row of Vs and is flat; the back is bumpy. Starting with the last chain completed (from the top), count every V, or stitch. Do not count the loop on the hook or the slip knot.

TIP: When your pattern calls for a long starting chain, work a few extra chain stitches. You won't have to start over if your count was off, and you can pick the extras out later by "unworking" them from the starting end.

Chain stitch

Yarn Over (yo)

Wrapping the yarn over the hook and catching it with the hook is called a yarn over, often abbreviated as yo.

Slip Stitch (sl st)

A slip stitch is made the same as a chain, and it is connected to the work. It is often used to join rounds or rows or to work across stitches without having to cut the yarn and start again.

- Insert the hook into the first stitch of the foundation chain. Yarn over and draw the yarn through both the stitch and the loop on the hook.
- Continue working into each chain stitch of the foundation to the end, but not the slip knot.

Single Crochet (sc)

The single crochet stitch is a short stitch that creates a thick, dense fabric with a woven look.

- To work a row of single crochet into the foundation chain, insert the hook into the second chain stitch from the hook. Yarn over and draw the yarn through the stitch.

- You now have two loops on the hook. Yarn over again and draw the yarn through both loops, ending with one loop on the hook.
- Continue working into each chain stitch of the foundation to the end, but don't work into the slip knot. This makes one row of single crochet stitches.

TIP: Stop and count to make sure you have the correct number of stitches.

- To work the next row of stitches, first make one chain stitch at the beginning of the row. Next, turn the work counterclockwise to work back across the row. In single crochet, this turning chain is not counted as a stitch—it is for placement only. When working back and forth in single crochet, you do not work into this turning chain.

TIP: Turning an item to work back across a row is commonly shortened to "turn."

- Working back across the row, insert the hook under both loops of the first stitch (the last stitch of the previous row).
- Yarn over and draw through the two stitch loops. Yarn over again, and pull yarn through both loops on the hook. Continue across the

COMMON STITCH PATTERNS

| single crochet | reverse single crochet | half-double crochet | double crochet | triple crochet |

row, working into both loops of each stitch. Be sure to work into the last stitch.

To count stitches, place your work on a flat surface and count the vertical part of each stitch. The vertical part of a stitch is also called the "post."

Reverse Single Crochet

This stitch is also known as crab stitch, and it results in a decorative corded edge. There are lots of names for this stitch. It can be called backwards single crochet, corded edge, rope stitch, Russian stitch, lobster stitch, and shrimp stitch. It is worked in the opposite direction from the usual direction. For right-handed people, reverse single crochet is worked from left to right; the stitch is worked from right to left for left-handed workers. This takes a little

practice, as it is awkward at first, but the created edge is lovely.

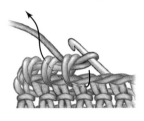

- To work a row of stitches, first work a row of regular single crochet stitches to keep the edge flat. Don't turn at the end of the row. Switch to a hook one size smaller and chain 1. Insert the hook into the next stitch to the right, hook the yarn, and draw a loop through the stitch to the front for two loops on the hook. Yarn over and draw the yarn through the two loops. Continue across the row.

TIP: The corded effect is more pronounced and attractive if reverse single crochet is worked

with the right side facing you. For a crisp corner, chain 1 between the two straight edges.

Half-double Crochet (hdc)

This is the first stitch that is worked by looping the yarn over the hook before inserting it into the work. These additional loops create stitches with more height. The yarn can be looped once, twice, or more times to create taller stitches. Half-double crochet is one of my favorite stitches. It's easy to work and makes a nice fabric that is dense and not too loose.

Half-double crochet stitches create a moderately dense fabric that is in between the single and double crochet stitches in height. The difference in height from single crochet changes how you work the first row and the number of turning chains. The first half-double crochet stitch is worked into the third chain of the foundation chain. The turning chain beginning of the next row requires two chain stitches. When working this stitch, you will work in the top of the turning chain after the first row.

Reverse single crochet creates a lovely edge.

- To work half-double crochet into a chain stitch, yarn over, insert the hook in the third chain from the hook, yarn over, and draw yarn through the stitch. Three loops are on the hook.

- Yarn over and draw yarn through all three loops so you have one loop remaining on the hook.
- Repeat in each chain stitch of the foundation but not the slip knot. This is the first row of half-double crochet. To start the next row, chain 2 to make a turning chain that raises the level of the hook and yarn to the correct height. Turn the work counterclockwise to work back across the row.

Unlike single crochet, the turning chain for half-double crochet counts as a stitch in this and other stitches. That means you will work the first stitch into the next-to-last stitch of the previous row because the turning chain is the first stitch.

If you work into the first stitch as well, you will add stitches. Missing the stitch in the turning chain will decrease the number of stitches on each row and the work will become narrower. Count your stitches to be sure until you get the hang of it.

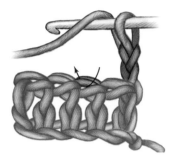

- Working back across the row, yarn over and insert the hook under both loops of the second stitch (the next-to-last stitch of the previous row).
- Continue across the row, working into both loops of each stitch. When you reach the end of the row, be sure to work a stitch into the top chain stitch of the turning chain from the previous row.

Double Crochet (dc)

Double crochet stitches are tall and create a more open fabric than single or half-double stitches. The height means three turning chains are necessary. The first double crochet is worked into the fourth chain stitch from the hook when working into the foundation. The

beginning of this stitch is the same as half-double crochet.

- To work double crochet into a chain stitch, yarn over, insert the hook in the fourth chain from the hook, yarn over, and draw yarn through the stitch. Three loops are on the hook.

- Yarn over and draw yarn through two loops so you have two loops remaining.

- Yarn over and draw through the remaining two loops, leaving one on the hook. This completes one double-crochet stitch.
- Repeat all of the steps in each chain stitch of the foundation, working into each chain instead of skipping four stitches. This is the first row of double crochet.

Stitch Height and Turning Chains

Turning chains are necessary at the beginning of a new row to raise the yarn to the correct height. If not, the edge of the work will be distorted or you will not have the proper stitch count. See the diagram for the stitches and their turning chains.

triple crochet
double crochet
half-double crochet
single crochet
slip stitch

4 3 2 1

- To start the next row, chain 3 to make a turning chain that raises the level of the hook and yarn to the correct height. Turn the work counterclockwise to work back across the row.
- Working back across the row, yarn over and insert the hook under both loops of the second stitch (the next-to-last stitch of the previous row). Continue across the row, working into both loops of each stitch. When you reach the end of the row, work a stitch into the top chain stitch of the turning chain from the previous row.

Triple Crochet (tc)

Triple crochet, sometimes called treble crochet, is one of the tallest crochet stitches. It creates an open, loose fabric. The height of this stitch requires four turning chains. The first triple crochet is worked into the fifth chain stitch from the hook when working into the foundation.

- To work triple crochet along the foundation, yarn over twice, insert the hook in the fifth chain stitch from the hook, yarn over, and draw yarn through the stitch. You should have four loops on the hook.

- Yarn over and draw yarn through two loops so you have three loops remaining.

- Yarn over and draw through the two loops, leaving two loops still on the hook.

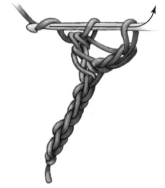

- Yarn over and draw through the remaining two loops, leaving one on the hook.

TIP: Triple crochet requires two yarn overs before inserting the hook into the work. Wrap the yarn around the thick part of the hook to keep the loops the correct size.

- Repeat in each chain stitch of the foundation but not the slip knot. This makes one row of triple crochet. Start the next row with chain 4 as a turning chain. Turn the work counterclockwise so it is in position to work back across the row.
- Working back across the row, yarn over twice and insert the hook under both loops of the second stitch and continue as described above. Work a stitch into the top chain stitch of the turning chain from the previous row.

JOINING NEW YARN

Start a new ball of yarn at the edge if you can (sometimes this isn't possible). No matter which stitch you are working, the method is the same. Work until there are two loops left on the hook, yarn over with the new yarn and pull it through both loops on the hook. Continue with the new yarn.

To change colors within a row, follow the same procedure. Just remember to start the new color when there are two loops left of the old color. Change colors this way even at the end of rows and rounds. Otherwise, the color change will not be crisp.

Work in Rounds

You can work in rounds, as well as back and forth in rows. If you crochet around a central point, you can create circles, squares, and tubes. This is the basis of working many types of patterns, such as granny squares and other motifs. *Motif* is pattern language for separate crocheted elements—square, circular, or some other shape—that are then joined to make a larger design.

- Start with a crocheted chain and join the ends of the chain with a slip stitch to form a ring. This is the ring referred to when pattern instructions say "join to form ring." Your pattern will specify the number of chains and stitches to work in the first round.

- After the slip stitch join, chain the required number to raise the yarn to the correct height for the first round. Work the first round into the ring by inserting the hook through the ring instead of the foundation chain.

When you reach the end of the first round, you may join the last stitch in the round to the first stitch with a slip stitch. This is closing the round, and you will then make a chain to start the next round. If the work is not joined, you will be working in a continuous spiral round. Be sure to place a marker in the last stitch of the round and move it on each subsequent round to keep track of the beginning of the rounds.

Working in rounds makes flat circles, squares, or other shapes, as long as the rounds have the proper number of increases to keep the work flat. If you find your flat circles and squares aren't flat, look closely and try these fixes:

- If the piece is curling or cupping into a bowl shape, it generally means the outside edge is too tight. Check that you have made the right number of increases. If the number of stitches is correct, they may be worked too tightly. Try reworking the increase rounds with a larger hook.
- If the work is ruffling, that is often a sign of too many stitches or stitches too loosely made. Either make fewer increases or try a smaller hook. Don't be

afraid to adjust stitches or hook sizes to get the result you want.

If you stop increasing and work around on the same number of stitches, you will make a tube. Tubes are useful for making socks, hats, and toys.

Increasing and Decreasing

Adding and subtracting stitches is simple and straightforward in crochet. Increasing stitches widens the fabric, and decreasing stitches narrows the fabric. This is called shaping, and it allows you to manipulate the fabric and make more complex projects, such as hats and sweaters.

Increasing

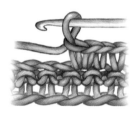

To increase, work two or more stitches into one stitch. You may do this at the edge of row or in the middle of the row. Your pattern will usually specify where to make an increase. The instructions may look something like "3dc in next stitch."

Increasing and decreasing

Increasing many stitches at the beginning of a row is accomplished by chaining the required number plus the turning chain and working back across these new stitches.

To increase a large number of stitches at the end of a row, you will create stitches by working into the sides of the previous stitch. Insert the hook into the lower left-most loop of the stitch just made and create a stitch. Continue working into the side of each stitch until the required number of stitches has been made.

TIP: The added stitches are usually the same type as those already in the row.

Shell Stitches

Shells (sometimes called fans) and V-stitches are made by working multiple stitches into one stitch as a group. The base is crowded into one place and the top spreads out into a shell or fan shape. They are usually worked with an uneven number of stitches and can have a chain space in the center. There are many variations of shell patterns, and they can be worked with any number or types of stitches. This family of patterns is one of the most distinctive and beautiful groups in crochet.

Corners

Keep a corner flat with an outside edge that is longer than the inside. To do this, add stitches in the corners to increase the distance along the outer edge. When working in single or half-double crochet, work three stitches into each corner stitch and mark the center stitch. On the next row, work three stitches into the marked stitch.

If you are working double crochet, work five stitches into the corners. If you find this corner to be too sharp, try three stitches instead. To keep the corner really sharp, use a slightly taller stitch for the middle stitch. For example, use a half-double instead of a single crochet, or a triple instead of a double.

Decreasing

A decrease is worked by partially completing two stitches and then combining them to create one stitch. Work the stitch to be decreased until just before there are two loops on the hook (the last step). Leave the loops on the hook and work the next stitch in the same way. Yarn over and draw through all loops on the hook.

Decrease in Single Crochet (sc2tog)

- Insert hook and pull up loop in each of next two stitches.

- Yarn over and pull through 3 loops on hook.

Decrease in Half-double Crochet (hdc2tog)

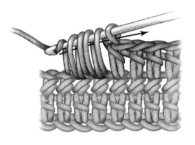

- Yarn over, insert hook and pull up a loop in each of next two stitches.

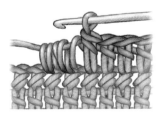

- Yarn over and pull through 5 loops on hook.

Decrease in Double Crochet (dc2tog)

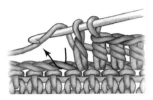

- Yarn over, insert hook, pull up a loop, yarn over and pull through 2 loops in each of next two stitches.

- Yarn over and pull through 3 loops on hook.

TIP: To decrease with a turning chain at the beginning of a row, make the chain first, and then work the decrease over the next two stitches.

Fastening Off

When you have completed the last crochet stitch of your piece, one loop will remain on the hook. To fasten this loop and prevent the stitches from unraveling, leave a tail of yarn at least 6 in. (15cm) long (or longer if you will be using it to sew a seam), cut the yarn, yarn over, and pull the end through the loop.

Working with Yarn Ends

Love lots of stripes, but don't love the yarn ends? Work them in as you stitch. When starting a new round in a new color, leave about 6 in. (15cm) of the old color. Hold the tails of both colors at the base of the next stitch. When inserting your hook to make the next stitch, work around the tails. Continue until the ends are secure, and trim them later.

Weaving in Ends

Once all work is done, the yarn ends should be woven in for a neat finish. When you're done crocheting, leave at least 6 in. (15cm) of yarn at the end. Don't cut ends short or rely on a knot to hold, as they work loose and can start unraveling. With some foresight, you can even leave yourself extra long ends where they can be used to make seams.

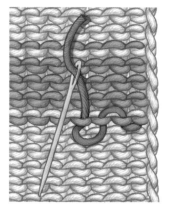

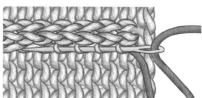

Thread the remaining yarn through a tapestry needle and weave it in and out of a wrong side row for at least 2 in. (5cm) or along a seam edge. If possible, thread the ends into the same color work. Be careful not to pull so tightly that the fabric puckers. Check the right side to see if the end shows and trim the excess yarn when finished.

To keep slippery ends in place, leave longer ends (8 in./20cm) and work them in diagonally through the back of several stitches one way, and then back diagonally the other way. Tack down the ends with matching sewing thread or even a small dot of fabric glue.

Left-handed Crochet

Crochet instructions and techniques work no matter whether you hold the hook in your left or right hand. To work left-handed, hold the hook in your left hand and the yarn in your right hand. You will then work from left to right. If you are watching someone who is right handed, sit opposite the person to watch instead of looking over his or her shoulder. To follow illustrations for right-handed crochet, look at them in a mirror.

Other than reversing the direction of work, working with your left hand is the same as with the right. All other instructions and techniques, such as turning chains and increases/decreases, are the same. Specific patterns will be reversed, such as shaping of left and right sides and symbol crochet rows.

Here are some left-handed diagrams for chain stitch and single crochet. The additional basic stitches, half-double, double and triple crochet, build on the skills used in the chain and single crochet. Once you've mastered these, you will be able to continue with the standard instructions.

TIP: Try working right-handed. You may find that you are able to crochet with the hook in your right hand with your left hand controlling the yarn.

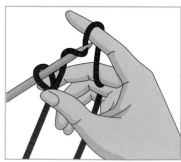

Chain

Single crochet

FINISHING

Careful finishing makes a big difference in how well your projects turn out. *Finishing* is really a set of skills and not just a few lines of instructions. The basic information here is a sound start, but there are more in-depth sources listed in the resources section. Be sure to practice new techniques and ask for help when in doubt.

Picking Up Stitches

This is a common technique for finishing edges and is often included as part of the finishing instructions for an item. It is used to begin working a section such as a neckband or border directly from the edge of a crocheted piece, thus avoiding having to join it with a seam.

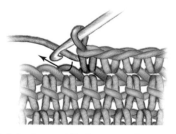

Picking up stitches on the top

When picking up stitches along a crochet edge, your first concern is where to insert the hook. Start with the right side of the work facing you. Pick up one stitch for each stitch in the pattern along the top edge of work of the same gauge. The bottom edge of the same piece is similar, except you will pick up one stitch for each chain in the foundation.

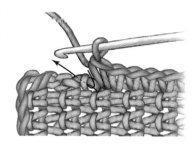

Picking up stitches on an edge

Picking up along a side edge requires more care. Be sure to insert the hook into a stitch and not the space between them. Working into the space creates unsightly holes. To space the stitches evenly along the edge, try this method. Lay the work on a flat surface, divide it evenly into four or eight sections, and mark with pins or markers. Divide the number of stitches to pick up by the same number and pick up the result from each section.

TIP: This is where your swatch comes in. Practice picking up stitches on it to get a feel for where to insert the hook and how to space the stitches. The first row of picked-up stitches is the key to an attractive edge. Make sure you are happy with how that row looks. Don't be afraid to pull it out and tweak it if necessary.

Blocking

Blocking is the process of using moisture and sometimes heat to smooth and shape the crocheted pieces to the correct size and shape before assembly. Blocking sets the stitches and can enhance the drape and feel of the fabric. It makes it easier to sew seams and finish edges and can adjust minor sizing problems. But blocking can't work miracles, and it won't correct major problems with size or gauge. Most items will benefit

from blocking to some degree. Many items do not need any blocking at all, and certain yarns, such as acrylic, do better with just laundering. Check the yarn label; some novelty yarns should not be blocked or pressed.

To wet-block a crocheted piece, lay it out on a large, flat, padded surface, and use rust-resistant pins to pin the pieces around the edges to the proper size according to the pattern. (Be sure the pins you use are rustproof—rust stains don't come out.) Use a spray bottle to wet the item, patting it gently to ensure the work is thoroughly damp. Leave the item pinned to the board until completely dry.

To steam-block, lay the piece out as described above. Use a warm iron and a damp pressing cloth or a steam iron. Don't use the iron directly on the surface, and don't press the fabric. Pass the iron lightly over the damp press cloth or the surface of the work, letting the steam penetrate the item. Leave the piece pinned flat until it is cool and dry.

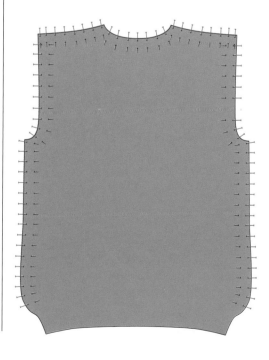

Seaming

To sew seams, you will need a blunt-tipped needle such as a bodkin or tapestry needle with an eye large enough for the seaming yarn. To pin the pieces together, use long pins with large heads. Insert the pins at right angles to the edges. (You can use safety pins to secure the fabric, too.)

Use the yarn you worked the pieces with to sew them together. If you used a novelty yarn that will be hard to sew with, use a smooth strong yarn in a matching or compatible color. Be sure that the seaming yarn has the same cleaning requirements as the rest of the project. An 18-in. (46cm) length of yarn is plenty. Pulling the yarn repeatedly through the fabric can cause it to break if it is too long.

Mattress Stitch

Mattress stitch is also referred to as working an "invisible seam," as the seam is very flat, smooth, and flexible to blend with the fabric.

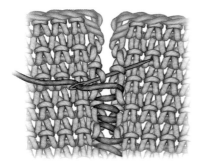

- Working from the right side, insert a yarn needle vertically under and out of a stitch on one piece and then under and out of a stitch exactly opposite on the other piece. Be sure to keep your seams straight by always inserting your needle in the same place along the seam. Move up a row on the first piece and stitch under the next stitch on that side, then under

the corresponding stitch on the second piece.

- Continue working up each side until you have a ladder of yarn approximately 1-in. (2.5cm) long, and then pull the yarn snug. Keep an even tension on the seam. Pull the yarn snug but not so tight that the edge or seam puckers. Try to leave a little "give" in the sewing yarn, as this reduces the chance that it will break and makes a more comfortable seam.
- At the beginnings and ends of seams, weave the yarn tails back into the seam and cut the yarn close to the work.

Slip Stitch and Single Crochet Seams

Both slip stitch and single crochet are useful ways to join your work. The resulting seam is strong and attractive. Both methods are generally worked from the wrong side of the fabric.

Slip stitch seam

- Hold the pieces to be joined with right sides together. Insert the hook through both loops of both edge stitches. Yarn over and pull the yarn through to make a slip stitch. Continue working along the edge, stopping to check the tension of the seam. Slip-stitch seams can be very tight and may pull the work in.

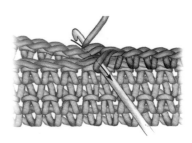

Single crochet seam

- A single-crochet seam is bulkier than slip stitch, but it has the advantage of being more flexible. Make it the same as the slip stitch seam except with single crochet stitches. Working from the right side results in a more pronounced and decorative seam.

Buttons and Buttonholes

Buy your buttons before making the buttonholes, and test your buttonhole method on your swatch to make sure it will work. When choosing buttons for crochet items, keep the size, style, and weight of the garment in mind. Bulky coats require large buttons, while light and lacy cardigans need delicate buttons. Stick with smooth buttons that don't have very irregular edges, which will cause them to snag on the garment.

Try different sizes and types of buttonholes to find one that fits the button and looks good on the garment. Most patterns include specific instructions for where and how to make buttonholes, but it's a good idea to check the buttonhole placement and spacing for yourself. Traditionally, buttonholes are on the right front of a garment for women and left front for men. Top and bottom buttonholes are ½–1 in. (1.2–2.5cm) from the top and bottom edge and evenly spaced in between.

Chain-and-Skip Buttonhole

The most common buttonhole is worked as part of a finishing band by chaining and skipping a number of stitches. The length of the buttonhole depends on the number of stitches skipped. This works well in single and half-double crochet bands, but may be too loose for taller stitches.

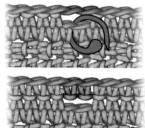

- Place a marker for buttonhole location, work to the marked stitch, chain 1–3 stitches, skip the same number of stitches as in the chain, and work to the next buttonhole. Repeat for all buttonholes. On the next row or round, work the same number of stitches into the space as skipped for the buttonhole.

Chain-Loop Buttonhole

The chain-loop buttonhole is easy to make and place as well as easy to size for any button. It is worked on the last row of an edge so you can adjust the button sizing and placement after the garment is finished. This technique works best with smaller buttons.

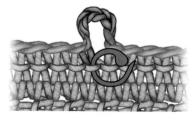

- Place a marker for buttonhole location, work to the marked stitch, chain the smallest number of stitches that will stretch slightly around your button, work in the next stitch (do not skip stitches), and continue along the edge.

EMBELLISHMENTS

Embellishment is the perfect way to add your own personality to your work or, if the project is a gift, to make it truly distinctive by incorporating something special to the recipient. These added details make your projects unique and set them apart from mass-produced store-bought pieces.

The variety of embellishment you can choose from is staggering! Buy beads, buttons, cords, ribbons, beaded trims, and appliqués at fabric and craft stores, and make handmade tassels, embroidery, and fringe—the possibilities are endless! When choosing embellishments for your handwork, there are a few points to keep in mind. They must be lightweight or the fabric could stretch and sag. Check that the embellishments won't snag or pull the fabric. Lastly, be sure the cleaning methods are compatible for both trim and fabric or that the trim is removable for cleaning.

Tassels

Large and small, beaded and plain—tassels can be made from all types of fibers and can be quite elaborate.

- Cut a piece of cardboard 2-in. (5cm) wide and as long as you want the tassel. Wrap the yarn around the cardboard lengthwise. The more wraps, the larger your tassel will be.

- Use a yarn needle to thread a length of yarn under the wrapped yarn, at the edge of the cardboard. Pull tightly and tie firmly. This is the top of your tassel.

- Cut yarn at the bottom. Remove the cardboard.

- Tie a length of yarn around the neck of the tassel.

Make tassels from all sorts of fibers.

Fringe

Fringe is a classic embellishment option. Try adding fringe to scarves, skirts, or blankets.

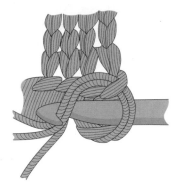

- Cut yarn twice the desired length, with extra for knotting, and fold the yarn in half over a crochet hook. From the wrong side of the work, insert the hook from front to back through a stitch. Pull the yarn ends through the stitch and loop; tighten. Finish all fringe before trimming to the desired length.

Felting

Felting is an old technique that changes the basic shape and structure of crocheted items. Technically, because it involves already-spun yarns made into fabric, this technique is called *fulling*. True felting starts with unspun wool fibers that are felted together to make a usable fabric. We will use the more common term, *felting*, in this book.

Why Wool Felts

The process starts with yarns made of animal fibers that have no special treatments to prevent felting. A felted project is usually started by working at a loose gauge to produce an item that is substantially larger than the finished dimensions. The shrinking and felting is now most often done in a washing machine. Felting may be done by hand in the same manner but is significantly more work.

Wool felts because the fibers are encased by microscopic scales. When the scales are smooth and lying flat, the fiber is equally smooth and tangle-free. Wool has the same structure as human hair. When the scales are roughed up by chemical, thermal, or mechanical agents, the fibers mat and shrink together. The agents that cause felting are soap (chemical), hot water and sudden temperature changes (thermal), and agitation (mechanical). Once the fibers have matted together, the process is irreversible.

How to Felt

It's a good idea to put your crocheted item in a zippered bag to collect the fuzz it will release. This fuzz is a by-product of the felting process, and it can damage your washing machine's water pump. Set the washing machine cycle for the lowest water level (smallest load) and heavy cycle (roughest agitation), and use the hottest water you can. Use a very small amount of laundry soap; begin with just a tablespoon or two.

Start the washer and add your bagged project. You might want to add something to help roughen it up as the washer agitates—old jeans are a great choice. Don't use towels, as they can leave little bits of fuzz on your project.

Let the washer agitate for about five minutes and check on your project. You may find that the items haven't felted or have even gotten a bit larger. Not to worry—this is the early phase of the process when the scales are opening up and the heat and water are being absorbed into the fibers. Let the machine continue to work its magic and keep checking every 5–10 minutes until your project is thoroughly felted.

Then, let the washer continue on with the rinse and spin operations. If you are concerned that any further felting will be too much, do not let the machine agitate the item. Swish it by hand in the tub and then spin the water out.

Blocking Felted Items

Wet wool items, whether felted or not, can be shaped easily. Push and pull flat items into shape and dry flat. Use head-sized bowls for hats and plastic bags to stuff purses. Leave projects undisturbed until they completely dry. Finish with a light brushing and a trim for stray fibers and fuzz.

Crocheted swatch before and after felting

Projects

Wearables

Simply Soft Scarf
Chic Kerchief
Classic Neck & Wrist Warmers
Beautiful Brimmed Hat
Feminine Floral Scarf
Strappy Cami
Lacy Wrap Overskirt
Wrap Around Shawl

Simply Soft Scarf

Make an easy and lovely scarf for cold weather. Finish the ends with tassels, or use your imagination and personalize the scarf. Give one as a gift to anyone on your list!

Finished Size:
Approximately 6 in. x 60 in. (15.2cm x 1.5m) before finishing.

Techniques and Skills Used:
Chain *(p. 17)*, **single crochet** *(p. 18)*

Project Gauge:
15 stitches/6 in. (15cm) over pattern stitch

Note: Gauge is not critical—it's a scarf, after all! Just make sure the fabric is soft and drapes well.

Materials:
- **Yarn:** 53% wool, 47% acrylic blend bulky-weight yarn, 100 yd. (92m) per skein, shaded or ombre colors, 2 skeins per scarf
- **Crochet hook:** size N (9mm) or size needed for gauge
- **Sew-on beaded trim:** 12 in. (30cm)
- **Tapestry or yarn needle**
- **Sewing needle and matching thread**
- **Tape measure**
- **Scissors**

Finishing:
Tassels *(p. 27)*

Note: Two basic stitches are used to make the entire scarf. There is no shaping and minimal finishing.

Pattern Stitch:
The pattern stitch is worked over a multiple of 2 stitches plus 1.
- Ch 16.
- **Row 1:** Sc in 2nd ch from hook, sc in each ch across, ch 2, turn.
- **Row 2:** Sc in 3rd sc of previous row, * ch 1, sk 1 sc, sc in next sc, repeat from * across, end with sc in turning ch of previous row, ch 1, turn
- **Row 3:** * Sc in next ch 1 space, sc in next sc, repeat from * across, end with sc in turning chs of previous row, ch 2, turn.
- Repeat rows 2 and 3 for pattern.
Swatch measures 6 in. (15cm) wide.

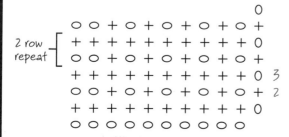

YARN AND SUBSTITUTION INFORMATION

The yarn chosen for this project is a thick, light wool and acrylic blend. Yarn label information suggests a knit gauge of 13 stitches to 4 in. (10cm) on size 11 (8mm) knitting needles. It is a very lightly spun yarn with thick-and-thin portions. The surface is not fuzzy.

You can choose a bulky-weight yarn with little twist and lots of loft in either 100% wool, a blend, or even 100% acrylic, as long as the yarn is soft and fluffy. Avoid highly spun yarns, as they may not be very soft. Don't use yarns with a large amount of surface fuzz, such as mohair, because they may be difficult to use and will obscure the stitch pattern.

This scarf was made with a variegated yarn that shades softly from one color to another. To achieve the same effect, choose a yarn with a long color repeat. (A long color repeat has long lengths of the same color.)

What is Variegated Yarn?

Variegated yarn is multicolored yarn dyed in sections. Each section may appear in a repeated or random pattern.

SCARF

- Ch 15, leave an 8-in. (20cm) length for finishing.
- **Row 1**: Sc in 2nd ch from hook, sc in each ch across, ch 2, turn.
- **Row 2**: Sc in 3rd sc of previous row, * ch 1, sk 1 sc, sc in next sc, repeat from * across, end with sc in turning ch of previous row, ch 1, turn
- **Row 3**: * Sc in next ch 1 space, sc in next sc, repeat from * across, end with sc in turning chs of previous row, ch 2, turn.

TIP: Be sure to work into the turning chain at the end of each row, or your scarf will get narrower as you work.

- Repeat rows 2 and 3 until scarf measures approximately 60 in. (1.5m) or desired length.
- Fasten off, leaving an 8-in. (20cm) length for finishing.

Finishing

- Using yarn needle and tails, gather ends and secure yarn.

- Make two 4 in. (10cm) tassels (see p. 27). Using sewing needle and thread, attach bead trim to neck of tassel.
- Attach tassels to gathered ends of scarf.

Creative Options

* Choose medium or dark solid, tweed, or neutral-toned yarns to make scarves for all the men in your life.

* Spice up your scarf with bright, hot colors to add some sizzle to winter weather.

* Go for cozy comfort with a soft, fluffy yarn. Don't use super-fluffy yarn, or it will be hard to see stitches while you're working.

* Add fringe to the ends and sew on chunky beads for extra style.

Chic Kerchief

A must-have wardrobe accessory, these kerchiefs are casual and elegant.
Because this project is so flexible and can be made any size, it's a great take-along project. Use just one ball of luscious luxury yarn to make a great accessory.

Finished Size:
About 23 in. (58cm) long at top edge and 12 in. (30cm) long at center

Techniques and Skills Used:
Chain stitch *(p. 17)*, **triple crochet** *(p. 21)*

Finishing:
Attach buttons, tassels, and other embellishments
(p. 27)

Note: Two stitches are used to make the entire kerchief with a stitch pattern composed of triple crochet groups. The scarf is worked flat from the point and can be made any size. The shaping is part of the stitch pattern, and finishing is minimal.

Project Gauge:
4 tc groups/3½ in. (8.8cm) over pattern stitch

Note: Gauge is not critical for this project. Be sure that the gauge you obtain will produce a nice, comfortable drape. The finished size is easy to adjust.

Materials:
- **Yarn:** A variety of yarns, 1 skein per kerchief:
  Bamboo blend: 89% bamboo, 11% acrylic, 63 yd. (57m) per skein
  Metallic: 69% acrylic, 19% nylon, 12% polyester, 166 yd. (151m) per skein
  Beaded: 90% acrylic, 5% polyester, 5% PVC, 103 yd. (95m) per skein
  Chenille: 51% rayon, 45.4% cotton, 3.6% metallic, 93 yd. (85m) per skein
- **Crochet hooks:** sizes G–J (4–5.5mm) or size needed for gauge
- **Button:** ¾ in. (19mm)
- **Tapestry or yarn needle**
- **Sewing needle and thread**
- **Tape measure**
- **Scissors**

Note: The weight of the yarn will affect the drape and feel of your finished kerchief. Light worsted-weight yarns worked with a large hook size give soft results.

Pattern Stitch:
The pattern stitch is worked in triple crochet groups in rows with increases at each end.
- Ch 5.
- **Row 1:** 3 tc in beginning ch, ch 4, turn.
- **Row 2:** 3 tc into 1st tc, skip 2 tc, 4 tc in top of turning ch, ch 4, turn.
- **Row 3:** 3 tc into 1st tc, skip 3 tc, 4 tc in next space between tc group, ending with 4 tc in top of turning ch, ch 4, turn.
- **Row 4:** 3 tc into 1st tc, skip 3 tc, * 4 tc in next space between tc group, skip 4 tc group, repeat from * across, ending with 4 tc in top of turning ch, ch 4, turn.
- Repeat row 4 for pattern.
Swatch measures 3½ in (8.8cm) over row 4.

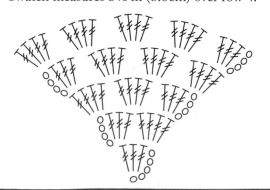

YARN AND SUBSTITUTION INFORMATION

The yarns chosen for this project are a mix of weights ranging from light worsted to heavy worsted. Yarn label information suggests knitting gauges ranging from 14 stitches to 4 in. (10cm), to 24 stitches to 4 in. (10cm), with size 5–10 (3.75–6mm) knitting needles. The characteristics of the yarns vary somewhat; one is a smooth and soft metallic, one has beads, and one is made from eco-friendly bamboo.

Almost any worsted-weight yarn that doesn't have too much surface texture will work for these kerchiefs. Stay away from slippery and fuzzy yarns, as they can be difficult to use. But if you fall in love with a ball of yarn and want a challenge, this is a good pattern to use because it is simple and only uses one ball of yarn.

Choose your hook size carefully. Make a swatch: Choose a likely hook size, use the label from your yarn as a guide, and start. Because the kerchief is made from the point, you will see quickly if you like how the project looks. If the triangle is too stiff, unravel the yarn and try a larger hook. If the fabric is too loose and floppy, rip it out and use a smaller hook.

Drape
Drape refers to the ability of a fabric to fall gracefully and form smooth folds.

KERCHIEF

- Ch 5.
- **Row 1:** 3 tc in beginning ch, ch 4, turn.
- **Row 2:** 3 tc into 1st tc, skip 2 tc, 4 tc in top of turning ch, ch 4, turn.
- **Row 3:** 3 tc into 1st tc, skip 3 tc, 4 tc in next space between tc group, ending with 4 tc in top of turning ch, ch 4, turn.
- **Row 4:** 3 tc into 1st tc, skip 3 tc, * 4 tc in next space between tc group, skip 4 tc group, repeat from * across, ending with 4 tc in top of turning ch, ch 4, turn.
- Repeat row 4 until top edge of scarf measures approximately 23 in. (58cm) or desired length to fit around head.
- End yarn and work ends in.

Finishing

- Using sewing thread and needle, attach button to corner of end row. Button into space at other corner for closure.
- Attach 3-in. (7.6cm) tassel to point, if desired (see p. 27).

Swap Your Yarn

Try a "yarn swap" and make a few of these kerchiefs at your next crochet circle. Ask everyone to bring a ball of yarn, or several, from their stash. Each person can choose a yarn and make a kerchief.

Creative Options

* The yarn you choose makes all the difference in the look and feel of these kerchiefs. A soft metallic yarn is dressy, and a natural linen or cotton is perfect for the beach.

* Just keep going! Make a shawl or cover-up by continuing in the pattern until the piece is as large as you like. (You will need more yarn.)

* These kerchiefs just beg to be embellished. Add beaded trims, ribbons, and even buttons to personalize your kerchief. Sew trims to the front edge for maximum impact.

Classic Neck & Wrist Warmers

These warmers offer a soft and feminine way to keep warm. The pretty edging can be worn framing your face or accenting your neckline. These great gifts are perfect for using up spare yarn.

Finished Size:
Wrist warmers, about 7–9 in. (18–23cm) circumference and 13 in. (33cm) long
Neck warmer, about 24 in. (61cm) circumference and 15 in. (38cm) long

Project Gauge:
22 stitches/5½ in. (14cm) in pattern stitch

Techniques and Skills Used:
Chain stitch (p. 17), **slip stitch** (p. 18), **single crochet** (p. 18), **double crochet** (p.20)

Materials:
- **Yarn:** 100% merino wool, worsted-weight yarn, 216 yd. (197m) per skein, 2 skeins
- **Crochet hook:** size K (6.5mm) or size needed for gauge
- **Tapestry or yarn needle**
- **Sewing needle and matching thread**
- **Size 6º crystal seed beads**
- **Tape measure**
- **Scissors**

Finishing:
Seaming (p. 26), **attaching beads**

Note: The body is worked flat in a textured stitch pattern with the edging formed from a decorative openwork stitch. There is no shaping.

Note: The yarns shown here are dyed to produce a soft, mottled effect within the solid colors. The process is called kettle dyeing, and it further enhances the texture of the stitch patterns in this project.

Pattern Stitch:
This stitch is worked over a multiple of 3 stitches plus 2, with 1 added for the beginning chain.
- Ch 24.
- **Row 1:** Skip 2 ch, * (1 sc, 1 ch, 1 dc) into next ch, skip 2 ch, repeat from *, ending 1 sc into last ch, ch 1, turn.
- **Row 2:** Skip 1st sc and next dc, * (1 sc, 1 ch, 1 dc) in next ch space, skip 1 sc and 1 dc, repeat from * ending with (1 sc, 1 ch, 1 dc) into last ch space, skip next sc, 1 sc into top of turning ch, ch 1, turn.
- Repeat row 2 for pattern.
Swatch measures 5½ in. (14cm) wide.

Edging Stitch:
- Work one row of sc after last pattern stitch row as a base row.
- **Row 1:** Ch 3, 2 dc into same sc, * 4 ch, skip 5 sc, 5 dc into next sc, repeat from *, ending with 3 dc in last sc, ch 2, turn.
- **Row 2:** * (3 dc, 3 ch, 3 dc) in first ch 4 arch, repeat from *, ending with dc in turning ch, end yarn off and work in ends.

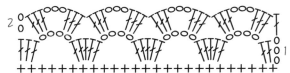

YARN AND SUBSTITUTION INFORMATION

The wrist and neck warmers are made of 100% merino wool. The yarn is worsted weight and soft with very little twist to the strand. Yarn label information suggests 4 to 5 stitches per inch (2.5cm) with needle sizes ranging from size 7–9 (4.5–5.5mm). The low twist gives the strand a slightly fuzzy surface with no shine. When choosing yarn for your warmers, look for soft, worsted-weight yarns made of wool or blends. The loft of this yarn gives the finished item a wonderful softness and warmth. The stitch pattern shows smooth or slightly textured yarns off nicely.

While a gentle color change works well, avoid strongly variegated colors because the color changes could overwhelm the stitch textures. Make a swatch to test your yarn if you're unsure.

Lofty Heights

Loft is the amount of air trapped inside a strand of yarn. High-loft yarn is springy and compressible, while low-loft yarn is firm and solid. The air spaces inside a high-loft yarn provide more insulation and keep you warmer.

WRIST WARMERS

- Ch 35.
- **Row 1:** Skip 2 ch, * (1 sc, 1 ch, 1 dc) into next ch, skip 2 ch, repeat from *, ending 1 sc into last ch, ch 1, turn.
- **Row 2:** Skip 1st sc and next dc, * (1 sc, 1 ch, 1 dc) in next ch space, skip 1sc and 1 dc, repeat from * ending with (1 sc, 1 ch, 1 dc) into last ch space, skip next sc, 1 sc into top of turning ch, ch 1, turn.
- Repeat row 2 for pattern until piece measures 12 in. (30cm). Do not break yarn, continue with edging pattern.

Edging

- Work one row sc across, increasing two stitches at each end (37 stitches).
- **Row 1:** Ch 3, 2 dc into same sc, * 4 ch, skip 5 sc, 5 dc into next sc, repeat from *, ending with 3 dc in last sc, ch 2, turn.
- **Row 2:** * (3 dc, 3 ch, 3 dc) in first ch 4 arch, repeat from *, ending with dc in turning ch, end yarn and work in all ends. Make 2 wrist warmers.

NECK WARMER

- Ch 98.
- **Row 1:** Skip 2 ch, * (1 sc, 1 ch, 1 dc) into next ch, skip 2 ch, repeat from *, ending 1 sc into last ch, ch 1, turn.
- **Row 2:** Skip 1st sc and next dc, * (1 sc, 1 ch, 1 dc) in next ch space, skip 1 sc and 1 dc, repeat from * ending with (1 sc, 1 ch, 1 dc) into last ch space, skip next sc, 1 sc into top of turning ch, ch 1, turn.
- Repeat row 2 for pattern until piece measures 14 in. (36cm). Do not break yarn, continue with edging pattern.

Increasing and Decreasing

You'll want to increase or decrease evenly across a row. Use a simple formula to calculates the number of stitches to work in between. Divide the number of stitches in the row by the number to increase or decrease plus one. In this project, the number of stitches on the last row is 96 and the number to increase is 6. Divide 96 by 7 (6 + 1 = 7) and round up to 14. This means you should increase 1 stitch every 14 stitches, adjusting as necessary to keep the shaping evenly spaced.

Edging

- Work one row sc across, increasing 6 stitches evenly spaced across (102 stitches). See "Increasing and Decreasing."
- **Row 1:** Ch 3, 2 dc into same sc, * 4 ch, skip 5 sc, 5 dc into next sc, repeat from *, ending with 3 dc in last sc, ch 2, turn.
- **Row 2:** * (3 dc, 3 ch, 3 dc) in first ch 4 arch, repeat from *, ending with dc in turning ch. End yarn and work in all ends.

Finishing

- **Wrist Warmers:** Sew side edges together. One of the holes in the edging makes a thumb opening.

- **Neck Warmer:** Sew side edges together.
- With sewing needle and matching thread, attach beads at intervals along scalloped edges and along first row of edging. Refer to photograph for placement.

Creative Options

* Work the body stitch pattern in one color, end the yarn, and continue the edging in a contrasting color.

* Choose a silk or silk-blend yarn, and accent with crystals for a dressy look. (The resulting fabric will drape nicely, but it will not be as warm.)

* Make a set in white with pearls and crystal beads for a winter bride.

* Explore other embellishment options, such as feather trim along the base of the edging.

Beautiful Brimmed Hat

Here's a versatile personal style statement that's easy to wear. Make a great accessory in sunny colors for summertime.

Finished Size:
Fits average adult, about 21 in. (53cm) circumference

Techniques and Skills Used:
Chain stitch (p. 17), **slip stitch** (p. 18), **single crochet** (p. 18), **reverse single crochet** (p. 19), **double crochet** (p. 20)

Project Gauge:
4 sc rounds/2 in. (5cm) in diameter

Materials:
- **Yarn:** 100% cotton worsted-weight yarn, 95 yd. (87m) per skein, self-striping shaded colors, 3 balls
- **Crochet hook:** size G (4mm), or size needed for gauge
- **Spray starch (optional)**
- **Sewing needle and matching thread**
- **Tapestry or yarn needle**
- **Tape measure**
- **Scissors**

Note: The sample project used all the stated yarn. Purchase an extra ball to make additional flower motifs.

Finishing:
Attach crochet flowers

Note: This hat is worked in the round. The crown and brim are shaped with increases. The edge is finished with reverse single crochet, and separate flower motifs are attached to the band.

Pattern Stitch:

The pattern stitch is simply single crochet worked in rounds. In joined single crochet rounds, the beginning chain 1 is not counted as a stitch. It's there to position the work for the next round. Do not count the joining slip stitch as a stitch, and do not work into it on subsequent rows.

- Ch 3.
- **Round 1:** 5 sc in 3rd ch from hook, sl st in top of beg ch.
- **Round 2:** Ch 1, 2 sc in each stitch around, sl st in 1st sc (12 sc).
- **Round 3:** Ch 1, * sc in 1st sc, 2 sc in next sc, repeat from * around, sl st in 1st sc (18 sc).
- **Round 4:** Ch 1, 1 sc in each sc around, sl st in 1st sc, end off. Swatch measures 2 in. (5cm) across.

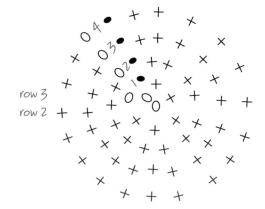

YARN AND SUBSTITUTION INFORMATION

The yarn chosen for this project is a moderately heavy 100% cotton yarn. Yarn label information suggests 20 stitches to 4 in. (10cm) with size 7 (4.5mm) needles. It is a moderately twisted yarn and has a matte surface.

Any yarns that can be worked into a firm fabric, such as acrylics and blends, will work well. Variegated self-striping colors lend interest to the simple stitches, but solid colors, especially in natural tones, give a sophisticated look.

Use textured yarns with care, as the texture may interfere with the look and function of the hat; make a swatch to be sure you like the effect. Avoid very soft yarns because they may not provide enough structure to be functional.

HAT
Crown

- Ch 3.
- **Round 1:** 5 sc in 3rd ch from hook, sl st in top of beg ch.
- **Round 2:** Ch 1, 2 sc in each stitch around, sl st in 1st sc (12 sc).
- **Round 3:** Ch 1, * sc in 1st sc, 2sc in next sc, repeat from * around, sl st in 1st sc (18 sc).

Finishing Edges

Reverse single crochet is also called "crab stitch," and it is often used to finish an edge. This stitch gives a neat and decorative finish (see p. 19).

- **Round 4:** Ch 1, 1 sc in each sc around, sl st in 1st sc.
- **Round 5:** Ch 1, * 1 sc in next 2 sc, 2 sc in next sc, repeat from * around, sl st in 1 sc (24 sc).
- **Round 6:** Ch 1, * 1 sc in next 3 sc, 2 sc in next sc, repeat from * around, sl st in 1 sc (30 sc).
- **Round 7:** Ch 1, *1 sc in next 4 sc, 2 sc in next sc, repeat from * around, sl st in 1 sc (36 sc).
- **Round 8:** Ch 1, 1 sc in each sc around, sl st in 1st sc.
- **Round 9:** Ch 1, * 1 sc in next   5 sc, 2 sc in next sc, repeat from * around, sl st in 1 sc (42 sc).
- **Round 10:** Ch 1, * 1 sc in next 6 sc, 2 sc in next sc, repeat from * around, sl st in 1 sc (48 sc).
- **Round 11:** Ch 1, * 1 sc in next 7 sc, 2 sc in next sc, repeat from * around, sl st in 1 sc (54 sc).
- **Round 12:** Ch 1, 1 sc in each sc around, sl st in 1st sc.
- **Round 13:** Ch 1, * 1 sc in next 8 sc, 2 sc in next sc, repeat from * around, sl st in 1 sc (60 sc).
- **Round 14:** Ch 1, * 1 sc in next 9 sc, 2 sc in next sc, repeat from * around, sl st in 1 sc (66 sc).
- **Round 15:** Ch 1, * 1 sc in next 10 sc, 2 sc in next sc, repeat from * around, sl st in 1 sc (72 sc).
- **Round 16:** Ch 1, * 1 sc in next 11 sc, 2 sc in next sc, repeat from * around, sl st in 1 sc (78 sc).
- **Round 17:** Ch 1, * 1 sc in next 12 sc, 2 sc in next sc, repeat from * around, sl st in 1 sc (84 sc).
- **Round 18:** Ch 1, * 1 sc in next 13 sc, 2 sc in next sc, repeat from * around, sl st in 1 sc (90 sc).
- **Round 19:** Ch 1, 1 sc in each sc around, sl st in 1st sc.

Creative Options

* Go wild with color and embellishment. Suit your fancy with extravagant beaded and feather trims for the band and brim.

* Neutral colors and natural fibers are perfect choices for the beach. Accent the hat with wooden beads or shell trims.

* Add silk flowers instead of crocheted flowers. Change the flowers for different occasions.

TIP: Working in spiral rounds makes a tube. It can be easier than making joined rounds when there is no shaping. Mark the beginning of the rounds with stitch markers to keep track of them.

Band

- Continue working around on 90 sc without joining rounds until piece measures approximately 5 in. (13cm) deep.

TIP: Try your hat on as it progresses to be sure the band is the length you like. You can adjust the depth of the band for your personal style. You may need more yarn for a longer band.

Brim

- At marked beginning of rounds, begin brim increase rounds and work joined rounds:
- **Brim round 1:** Ch 1, * 1 sc in next 14 sc, 2 sc in next sc, repeat from * around, sl st in 1 sc (96 sc).
- **Brim round 2:** Ch 1, * 1 sc in next 15 sc, 2 sc in next sc, repeat from * around, sl st in 1 sc (102 sc).

- **Brim round 3:** Ch 1, * 1 sc in next 16 sc, 2 sc in next sc, repeat from * around, sl st in 1 sc (108 sc).
- **Brim round 4:** Ch 1, * 1 sc in next 17 sc, 2 sc in next sc, repeat from * around, sl st in 1 sc (114 sc).
- **Brim round 5:** Ch 1, 1 sc in each sc around, sl st in 1st sc.
- **Brim round 6:** Ch 1, * 1 sc in next 18 sc, 2 sc in next sc, repeat from * around, sl st in 1 sc (120 sc).
- **Brim round 7:** Ch 1, * 1 sc in next 19 sc, 2 sc in next sc, repeat from * around, sl st in 1 sc (126 sc).
- **Brim round 8:** Ch 1, * 1 sc in next 20 sc, 2 sc in next sc, repeat from * around, sl st in 1 sc (132 sc).
- **Brim round 9:** Ch 1, * 1 sc in next 21sc, 2 sc in next sc, repeat from * around, sl st in 1 sc (138 sc).
- **Brim trim round:** Ch 1, work reverse sc around. End yarn and work ends in.

round. End off and work ends in. Work the 15 sc into the ring over the starting tail to save working it in later. Trim.
- Make 10.

Finishing
- Press hat and flowers well, and starch lightly if desired.
- Using sewing needle and thread, attach flowers to band at first and third petals, using photographs as a guide.

Dc2tog
Dc2tog means to work one double crochet into each of the next two single crochet stitches until one loop of each stitch remains on the hook. Yarn over and go through all three loops on the hook.

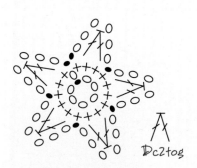

Flower Motifs
- Ch 6, slip stitch into first chain to form a ring.
- **Round 1:** Ch 1, 15 sc into ring, sl st into first sc.
- **Round 2:** (Ch 3, dc2tog, ch 3, sl st into next sc) five times with last sl st into first sc of previous

Feminine Floral Scarf

Make a modern scarf reminiscent of Irish-style crochet. The lacy filigree scarf is scattered with delicate flower motifs. Its fresh colors will liven up your spring wardrobe.

Finished Size:
About 5 x 60 in. (13cm x 1.5m) before finishing

Techniques and Skills Used:
Chain stitch *(p. 17)*, **slip stitch** *(p. 18)*, **single crochet** *(p. 18)*, **double crochet** *(p. 20)*

Techniques:
Join ring *(p. 21)*, **work in round** *(p. 21)*, **double crochet two together** *(p. 23)*

Project Gauge:
Mesh stitch: 8 meshes/ 5 in. (13cm), 3 rows/ 2 in. (5cm) over pattern stitch after pressing 1 flower measures 2 in. (5cm) across

Note: Press your swatch before measuring to make sure you have the correct gauge. This pattern stitch stretches significantly.

Finishing:
Attaching motifs

Materials:
- **Yarn:** 100% bamboo, worsted-weight yarn, 77 yd. (70m) per skein, 2 skeins for main color, 2 skeins for flowers
- **Crochet hook:** size G (4mm) or size needed for gauge
- **Tapestry or yarn needle**
- **Sewing needle and matching thread**
- **Tape measure**
- **Scissors**

Note: Irish crochet is traditionally worked in fine white cotton thread. Using worsted-weight yarn updates the look of this style of crochet.

Pattern Stitch:
Mesh Stitch:
- Ch 27.
- **Row 1:** Dc in 6th ch from hook (counts as turning chain and ch 2 space), * ch 2, skip 2 ch, dc in next ch, repeat from * across, dc in last ch, ch 5, turn.
- **Row 2:** Dc next dc, * ch 2, skip ch 2 space dc in next dc, repeat from * across, dc in 3rd ch of turning chain, ch 5, turn.
- Repeat row 2 for pattern.
Swatch measures 5 in. (13cm) wide.

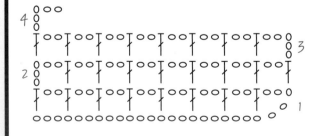

Flower:
- Ch 6, join to form ring.
- **Round 1:** Ch 1, work 15 sc into ring, slip stitch into first sc.
- **Round 2:** (Ch 3, dc2tog over next 2 sc, ch 3, sl st into next sc) 5 times.
- End yarn and work ends in. Flower measures 2 in. (5cm) across.

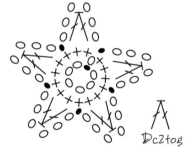

Note: Irish Crochet, generally worked with thread, was developed to resemble expensive needle lace. In true Irish crochet, floral motifs are worked first and the net or mesh fabric is worked to join them.

YARN AND SUBSTITUTION INFORMATION

The yarn used to make the scarf is a worsted-weight 100% bamboo yarn. Bamboo is a renewable fiber source. Yarn label information suggests 5 stitches to 1 in. (2.5cm) with a size 7 (4.5mm) needle. The yarn is very lightly twisted and has a soft sheen with no fuzziness. The yarn resembles silk in the skein.

Other good choices would be silk, a silk blend, cashmere, or fine merino wool. For a dressy look, choose yarns that are smooth with a soft sheen. Avoid highly textured yarns unless you want a more casual and bulky look. Lightweight mohair yarns may work as well, but make a swatch to make sure you like the finished look.

SCARF

- Ch 27.
- **Row 1:** Dc in 6th ch from hook (counts as turning chain and ch 2 space), * ch 2, skip 2 ch, dc in next ch, repeat from * across, dc in last ch, ch 5, turn.
- **Row 2:** Dc next dc, * ch 2, skip ch2 space dc in next dc, repeat from * across, dc in 3rd ch of turning chain, ch 5, turn.
- Repeat row 2 until scarf measures approximately 60 in. (1.5m) or desired length.
- Fasten off and work ends in.

Flowers

- Ch 6, join to form ring
- **Round 1:** Ch 1, work 15 sc into ring, slip stitch into first sc.
- **Round 2:** (Ch 3, dc2tog over next 2 sc, ch 3, slip stitch into next sc) 5 times.

Creative Options

* Try different color combinations or use just one color. All-black is a sophisticated and dressy choice for special occasions. Heathery yarns and flowers in autumn shades of plum, burgundy, gold, and rust are perfect for a crisp fall day.

* Sew crystal beads to the centers and petals of flowers for a dew-kissed look.

* Use variegated yarn for the mesh ground and make the flowers in coordinating solid colors.

* Make an extra flower and pin it to a headband or jacket.

- End yarn and work ends in.
- Make 27 flowers.

TIP: You can attach the flowers to the mesh as they are made. After the dc2tog at the top of the petal, work a slip stitch into the mesh background, and then continue as written.

Finishing

- Using sewing needle and thread, attach flowers to scarf as in illustration. Secure three or more points of each flower so they lie flat.

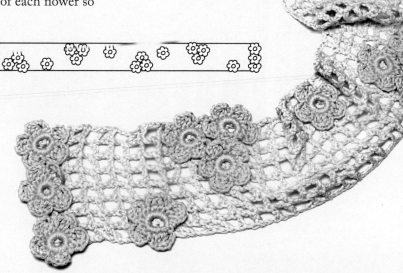

Strappy Cami

Here's a versatile personal style statement that's easy to wear. Make a great accessory in rich colors for summertime. This soft and feminine top is a great weekend project. Layer for warmth, or wear it alone for dressy occasions. A softly scalloped hem and delicate chain straps offer subtle detailing.

Finished Size:
34, 38, 42, 46 in. (86, 97, 107, 117 cm) at bust Directions are written for smallest size with larger sizes in parentheses.

Note: Allow approximately 2 in. (5cm) of ease for the camisole to fit properly. Too much ease, and the camisole will gap and sag; too little, and it will be snug and restricting.

Materials:
- **Yarn:** 50% alpaca, 50% Tencel, light worsted-weight yarn, 108 yd. per skein, 5 (5, 6, 7) skeins
- **Crochet hooks:** size J (5.5mm) or size needed for gauge over pattern and size F (3.754mm) for straps
- **Tapestry or yarn needle**
- **Tape measure**
- **Scissors**

Note: Tencel is a trademarked brand name for lyocel, which is a cellulose fiber produced from wood pulp.

Techniques and Skills Used:
Chain stitch *(p. 17)*, **single crochet** *(p. 18)*, **double crochet** *(p. 20)*

Finishing:
Seaming *(p. 26)*, **attaching straps**

Note: A double-crochet solid-shell pattern is worked flat for the body. There is no shaping and finishing includes sewing the center back seam and attaching chain straps.

Project Gauge:
4 shells/6 in. (15cm); 10 rows/4 in. (10cm) over pattern stitch.

Pattern Stitch:
The pattern stitch is worked over a multiple of 6 stitches plus 2.
- With larger hook, ch 26.
- **Foundation row:** Sc in 2nd ch and in each ch across, ch 1, turn.
- **Row 1:** Sc into 1st sc, * skip 2 sc, 5 dc in next sc, skip 2 sc, 1 sc in next sc, repeat from * across, ch 3, turn.
- **Row 2:** 2 dc into 1st sc, * skip 2 dc, 1 sc in next dc, skip 2 dc, 5 dc in next sc, repeat from * ending with 3 dc into last sc, ch 1, turn.
- **Row 3:** Sc in 1st st, * skip 2 dc, 5 dc in next sc, skip 2 dc, 1 sc in next dc, repeat from * ending with 1 sc in turning ch, ch 1, turn.
- Repeat rows 2 and 3 for 10 rows total.
Swatch measures 6 in. (15cm) wide and 4 in. (10cm) tall.

Note: In this shell pattern, you are simply alternating shells over single crochet stitches on alternate rows.

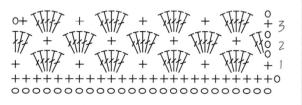

YARN AND SUBSTITUTION INFORMATION

The yarn chosen for this soft camisole is light worsted 50% alpaca, 50% Tencel yarn. Yarn label information suggests 5¼ stitches per inch (2.5cm) using size 6 (4mm) knitting needles. The yarn is lightly twisted with lovely sheen and a slight hairiness. The resulting fabric drapes very well.

When choosing a substitute yarn for this project, look for soft and flexible yarn to provide the right drape. Good fiber choices might be silk, linen, bamboo, nylon, or acrylic microfiber. Select cotton with care, as some yarns will be too stiff or coarse; work a swatch if you are unsure.

Unless you want a fuzzy caterpillar look, stay away from heavily textured or furry yarns because they will add bulk and obscure the delicate stitch pattern. Also, be sure to choose a yarn that is not too heavy or bulky because the weight would quickly overwhelm the garment.

Test Swatches

In addition to checking gauge, making swatches is a good way to check how yarns may behave before starting a garment.

CAMISOLE
Body (worked from the top edge down)

- With larger hook, ch 140 (152, 170, 188).
- **Foundation row:** Sc in 2nd ch and in each ch across, ch 1, turn.
- **Row 1:** Sc into 1st sc, * skip 2 sc, 5 dc in next sc, skip 2 sc, 1 sc in next sc, repeat from * across, ch 3, turn.
- **Row 2:** 2 dc into 1st sc, * skip 2 dc, 1 sc in next dc, skip 2 dc, 5 dc in next sc, repeat from * ending with 3 dc into last sc, ch 1, turn.
- **Row 3:** Sc in 1st st, * skip 2 dc, 5 dc in next sc, skip 2 dc, 1 sc in next dc, repeat from * ending with 1 sc in turning ch, ch 1, turn.

- Repeat rows 2 and 3 until piece measures 12 (12, 13, 14) in./30 (30, 33, 36) cm or desired length from beginning, end off.
- Work ends in.

Straps

- With smaller hook, work a chain 14 (15, 16, 17) in./35 (38, 41, 43) cm long. Leave 6 in. (15cm) tails at both ends.
- Make 6.

Finishing

- Sew back seam.
- Collect three chains into a group and attach each group to front 4 in. (10cm) from center front with a knot. Work ends into inside of work.
- Try on and attach straps individually to top edge of back with chains about 1 in. (2.5cm) apart within each group. Work ends in.

The Importance of Gauge

Take time to check the gauge for this project to make sure your finished camisole will fit properly.

Creative Options

* Use trim to embellish your top. Sew beads or appliqué trim along the top or bottom edge.

* Make bold or subtle stripes by alternating colors every one or two rows.

* Make a warm-weather strappy tank in silk or bamboo.

* Change the straps by making chains approximately 4 in. (10cm) longer. After determining the length, tie one or more knots to secure all chains together before attaching to back.

Lacy Wrap Overskirt

This stylish and easy skirt looks great over everything in your closet. Wear it over a swimsuit or shorts for a cool summer look, or layer over jeans, leggings, or a skirt for an evening out.

Finished Size:
About 35 (40, 44, 49) in./0.89 (1.0, 1.1, 1.2) m at top, excluding ties; 15 (15, 17, 17) in./38 (38, 43, 43) cm long. Instructions are written for size small, with larger sizes in parentheses.

Materials:
- **Yarn:** 75.9% cotton, 24.1% viscose, worsted-weight yarn, 60 yd. (55m) per skein, 7 (8, 9, 10) skeins
- **Crochet hook:** size J (5.5mm) or size needed for gauge
- **Tapestry or yarn needle**
- **Tape measure**
- **Scissors**

Techniques and Skills Used:
Chain stitch *(p. 17)*, **double crochet** *(p. 20)*

Finishing:
Pressing

Project Gauge:
3 pattern repeats/6½ in. (16cm)

Pattern Stitch:
The pattern stitch is worked over a multiple of 6 stitches plus 1. Add three to the base chain to start.
- Ch 22.
- **Row 1:** 2 dc in 4th ch from hook, * ch 1, sk 2 ch, dc in next ch, ch 1, sk 2 ch, (3 dc, ch 1, 3 dc) in next ch (shell made), repeat from * across, end 3 dc in last ch, ch 3, turn.
- **Row 2:** 2 dc in 1st dc, ch 1, skip 2 dc, * skip ch 1 space, 1 dc in next dc, ch 1, skip ch 1 space, 1 shell in next ch space, ch 1, repeat from * across, end 3 dc in turning ch, ch 3, turn.
- Repeat row 2 for pattern.
Swatch measures 6½ in. (16cm) wide.

Note: Crochet instructions usually give a detailed instruction to make a shell stitch. They will often say "shell made" and then simply refer to that unit as a shell in the rest of the pattern. This saves space and reduces the amount of text you need to read.

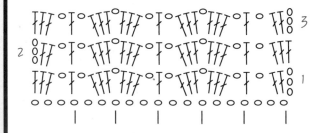

YARN AND SUBSTITUTION INFORMATION

The yarn chosen for this project is worsted-weight 75.9% cotton and 24.1% viscose yarn. Yarn label information suggests 4.5 stitches to 1 in. (2.5cm) using a size 7 (4.5mm) hook. It is a moderately twisted, slightly shiny cotton yarn. The textured viscose strand is wrapped around the cotton, so the overall effect is of texture and shine, but the yarn is not fuzzy or furry. Avoid highly textured or furry yarns, as the texture may obscure the stitch pattern and add bulk to the finished garment.

Other good choices would be cotton or cotton blends that work into a fabric with substantial drape and weight. Blends of natural fibers and synthetics are also possibilities. Choose strongly shaded yarns carefully, as the color changes can be distracting. Solid colors, especially natural tones, would be a sophisticated touch.

Shell Stitch

Two basic stitches are used together to make a shell stitch pattern. The skirt is worked flat and shaped by increasing stitches inside the shells.

A crochet shell is made by working a specified number of stitches into one stitch. Stitch patterns are formed by combining the shell with other stitches. Variations on this technique are endless and produce a lovely and distinctive family of crochet patterns.

SKIRT

- Ch 94 (106, 118, 130).
- **Row 1:** 2 dc in 4th ch from hook, * ch 1, sk 2 ch, dc in next ch, ch 1, sk 2 ch, (3 dc, ch 1, 3 dc) in next ch (shell made), repeat from * across, end 3 dc in last ch, ch 3, turn.
- **Row 2:** 2 dc in 1st dc, ch 1, skip 2 dc, * skip ch 1 space, 1 dc in next dc, ch 1, skip ch 1 space, 1 shell in next ch space, ch 1, repeat from * across, end 3 dc in turning ch, ch 3, turn.
- Repeat row 2 for 5 (5, 7, 7) more rows—7 (7, 9, 9) rows worked total.
- **Row:** 8 (8, 10, 10): 2 dc in 1st dc, ch 1, skip 2 dc, * skip ch space, 1 dc in next dc, ch 1, skip ch 1 space, (3 dc, ch 2, 3 dc) in next ch (shell made), ch 1, repeat from * across, end 3 dc in turning ch, ch 3, turn.

TIP: Row 8 (10) has a ch-2 space between the dc groups of the shell to allow room for the increase on row 9 (11).

- **Row 9 (9, 11, 11) Increase Row:** 2 dc in 1st dc, ch 1, skip 2 dc, * skip ch 1 space, 1 dc in next dc, ch 1, skip ch 1 space (4 dc, ch 2, 4 dc) in next ch (large shell made), ch 1, repeat from * across, end 3 dc in turning ch, ch 3, turn.

TIP: The larger shell makes the skirt flare attractively.

35 (40, 44, 49) in.
0.89 (1.0, 1.1, 1.2) m

15 (15, 17, 17) in.
38 (38, 43, 43) cm

Creative Options

✳ Make this skirt from natural cotton or linen yarn for a comfortable and eco-friendly beach cover-up.

✳ With such a busy stitch pattern, limit any extra embellishments. Add tassels or charms to the end of the ties, or attach beaded drops or dangles to the points of the shells along the hem for a festive look.

✳ Make the wrap in solid black or white silk, wear it over a sleek skirt, and really turn some heads!

- Work row 9 (9, 11, 11) eight more times (17, 17, 19, 19 rows worked total), end yarn and work all ends in.

Top Band

- Attach yarn at corner of beginning edge, ch 40.
- Sc in 2nd ch from hook and in each chain across.
- Continue across top of skirt, 1 sc in each foundation chain to end, ch 40.
- Sc in 2nd ch from hook and in each chain across.
- Upon reaching top of skirt, continue sc in each sc across both skirt and tie on other side.
- Work rows of sc across entire top and two ties until band measures 1½ in. (3.8cm).
- End yarn and work ends in.

Finishing

- Press skirt and ties carefully with a warm iron. Pull shells downward to open up lace pattern, and press from both sides.

TIP: Test iron temperature and pressing method on your swatch first.

Wrap Around Shawl

A lovely lace stitch pattern makes this easy-to-wear wrap special. Simple construction shows off the shaped edges and beautiful openwork.

Finished Size:
About 12 x 80 in.
(30cm x 2m)

Techniques and Skills Used:
Chain stitch *(p. 17)*,
single crochet *(p. 18)*,
double crochet *(p. 20)*

Finishing:
Working along edge, attach tassels or beads (optional) *(p. 27)*

Note: A variation of shell lace is worked flat from both sides of the foundation chain to make scallops. There is no shaping and finishing is minimal.

Materials:
- **Yarn:** 50% superfine alpaca, 50% wool, light worsted-weight yarn, 219 yd. (200m) per skein, 4 skeins
- **Crochet hook:** size J (5.5mm) or size needed for gauge
- **Coordinating beads for tassel drops (optional)**
- **Tapestry or yarn needle**
- **Sewing needle and matching thread**
- **Tape measure**
- **Scissors**

Project Gauge:
3 pattern repeats/6 in. (15cm)
5 rows/4 in. (10cm) at point of scallop

Note: The pattern gauge is not very important in this project. Check to be sure that you like the fabric you make and how it drapes. If your gauge varies significantly from the sample, you may need more or less yarn than specified.

Pattern Stitch:
The pattern stitch is worked over a multiple of 7 stitches plus 1.
- Ch 22.
- **Row 1:** 2 dc in 4th ch from hook, ch 1, * sk 2 ch, 1 dc in next ch, ch 1, sk 2 ch, (3 dc, ch1, 3 dc) in next ch, ch 1, repeat from *, ending with 3 dc in last ch, ch 3, turn.
- **Row 2:** 2 dc in 1st dc, ch 1, * 1 dc in next dc, ch 1, (3 dc, ch 1, 3 dc) in ch 1 space between previous 3 dc, ch 1, repeat from *, ending with 3 dc in top of turning chain, ch 3 turn.
- Repeat row 2 for pattern.
Swatch measures 6 in. (15cm) wide.

YARN AND SUBSTITUTION INFORMATION
The yarn chosen for this project is a light worsted-weight 50% superfine alpaca, 50% wool blend. Yarn label information suggests a knitting gauge of 5 stitches to 1 in. (2.5cm) with size 7 (4.5mm) needles. It is a lightly twisted yarn that has a hairy surface with little or no sheen.

To substitute another yarn, look for a soft yarn that drapes well. Natural fibers will add a luxurious look and feel to your shawl. Other good choices would be soft organic cottons or natural and synthetic fiber blends.

Strongly variegated colors may obscure the stitch patterns. If you want to use one of these yarns, make a large swatch first to test the effect. Highly textured yarns may interfere with the look and feel of the wrap.

SHAWL
First Half
- Ch 43.
- **Row 1:** 2 dc in 4th ch from hook, ch 1, * sk 2 ch, 1 dc in next ch, ch 1, sk 2 ch, (3 dc, ch 1, 3 dc) in next ch, ch 1, repeat from *, ending with 3 dc in last ch, ch 3, turn.
- **Row 2:** 2 dc in 1st dc, ch 1, * 1 dc in next dc, ch 1, (3 dc, ch 1, 3 dc) in ch 1 space between previous 3 dc, ch 1, repeat from *, ending with 3 dc in top of turning chain, ch 3, turn.

- Repeat row 2 until piece measures 40 in. (1m) or desired length.
- Cut yarn and work ends in.

Second Half
- Working in other side of foundation chain, attach yarn and start with row 1. Work as written until piece measures a total of 80 in. (2m) long.
- Cut yarn and work all ends in.

Finishing
- Attach yarn to long edge at corner and work one row of sc evenly along edge. Repeat for other edge.
- Block with steam and press carefully, pulling scalloped points into shape.

Optional Beaded Tassel Drops
- Using sewing needle and thread, string beaded drops into groups of three and attach to points of scallops.
- Alternatively, make and attach 3-in. (7.6cm) yarn tassels or fringe (p. 28) to the ends.

Working the Chain
To work on the opposite side of the chain, hold the piece so the starting chain is on top and the right side is facing you. Join the yarn at the right-hand corner and stitch into each loop on the other side of the chain as instructed in the pattern.

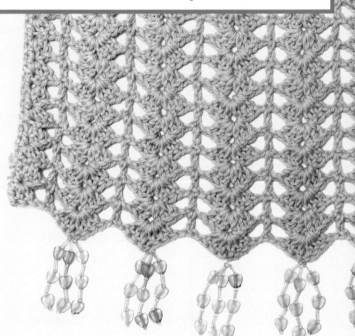

Creative Options

* Silk, bamboo, or fine cotton yarns are wonderful for a summertime shawl.

* Work alternate rows in different color stripes. White and cream shades are light and lovely, while black, charcoal, and silver hues are dramatic.

* Make a decorative throw for your sofa or bed by doubling the width with a starting chain of 85. Be sure to purchase plenty of yarn for the project.

Projects

For the Home

Shaped Market Bag
Casual Cushion
Not Your Granny's Rug
Get Organized Storage Baskets
Lacy Café Curtains
Table Runner & Place Mats
Felted Basket

Shaped Market Bag

R educe, reuse, recycle! Here's a stylish tote to help eliminate your need for plastic bags. Work it in a worsted yarn for a sturdy working bag, or use a sport-weight yarn for a more delicate and stylish alternative.

Finished Size:
About 12 in. (30cm) long, 25 in. (63cm) including handle

Techniques and Skills Used:
Chain stitch *(p. 17)*, **slip stitch** *(p. 18)*, **single crochet** *(p. 18)*, **half-double crochet** *(p. 19)*

Project Gauge:
Worsted Yarn:
Single crochet: 5 sc rounds/2½ in. (6.3cm) diameter
Mesh stitch: 8 meshes/6 in. (15cm), 3 rows/2¼ in. (5.7cm) over pattern stitch

Sport-weight Yarn:
Single crochet: 5 sc rounds/1¾ in. (4.4cm) diameter
Mesh stitch: 8 meshes/4½ in. (11cm), 3 rows/2 in. (5cm) over pattern stitch

Materials:
- **Yarn:** 100% cotton, worsted-weight yarn, 95 yd (87m) per skein, twisted colors, 3 balls
- **Crochet hooks:** size G (4mm) or size needed for gauge
- **Foam board or heavy cardboard:** about 6 in. (15cm) square for base (optional)
- **Tapestry or yarn needle**
- **Tape measure**
- **Scissors**

Note: Use 100% cotton sport-weight yarn, 100 yd. (91m) per skein, 3 balls, and a size F hook to make the smaller version. Feel free to change sizes to get the effect you want.

Finishing:
Attach tassel *(p. 27)*, **single crochet seam** *(p. 26)*, **press if desired**

Note: Single crochet is worked in rounds for the base, with double-crochet mesh worked in rounds up the sides of the bag. The handle is worked flat in single-crochet rows.

Pattern Stitch:
The pattern stitch is single crochet worked in rounds for the base and double-crochet mesh for the body.
- Ch 4, join with slip stitch to form ring.
- **Round 1:** 5 sc in ring, slip stitch in top of beginning ch.
- **Round 2:** Ch 1, 2 sc in each stitch around, sl st in 1st sc (12 sc).
- **Round 3:** Ch 1, * sc in 1st sc, 2sc in next sc, repeat from * around, sl st in 1st sc (18 sc).
- **Round 4:** Ch 1, 1 sc in each sc around, sl st in 1st sc.
- **Round 5:** Ch 1, * 1 sc in next 2 sc, 2 sc in next sc, repeat from * around, sl st in 1 sc (24 sc), end off.
Swatch measures 2½ in. (6.3cm) or 1¾ in. (4.4cm).

Mesh Stitch:
- Ch 27.
- **Row 1:** Dc in 6th ch from hook (counts as turning chain), * ch 2, skip 2 ch, dc in next ch, repeat from * across, dc in last ch, ch 5, turn.
- **Row 2:** Dc next dc, * ch 2, skip ch 2 space dc in next dc, repeat from * across, dc in 3rd ch of turning chain, ch 5, turn.
- Repeat row 2 for pattern.
Swatch measures 6 in. (15cm) or 4½ in. (11cm).

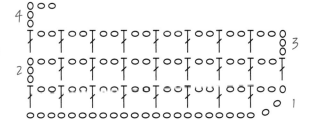

YARN AND SUBSTITUTION INFORMATION

The first yarn chosen for this project is a moderately heavy 100% cotton yarn. Yarn label information suggests 20 stitches to 4 in. (10cm) on size 7 (4.5mm) needles. It is a moderately twisted yarn with a matte surface. The yarn has little or no give.

The second sample was made with a cabled cotton lightweight yarn. Yarn label information suggests a knit gauge of 17 stitches to 4 in. (10cm) on size 7 (4.5mm) knitting needles. It is a well-cabled yarn with no variation in diameter along the length. The yarn surface is smooth and slightly shiny.

Other good choices would be any yarn that can be worked into a firm fabric, including acrylic and blends. A twist of color adds visual interest to the simple stitches.

Do not use highly textured yarns because the texture may interfere with the look and function of the bag. Avoid very soft yarns as they may not produce a bag with enough shape to be useful.

BAG

Base

TIP: Do not count joining slip stitch as a stitch, and do not work into it on subsequent rows.

- Ch 4, join with slip stitch to form ring.
- **Round 1:** 5 sc in ring, slip stitch in top of beginning ch.
- **Round 2:** Ch 1, 2 sc in each stitch around, sl st in 1st sc (12 sc).
- **Round 3:** Ch 1, * sc in 1st sc, 2 sc in next sc, repeat from * around, sl st in 1st sc (18 sc).
- **Round 4:** Ch 1, 1 sc in each sc around, sl st in 1st sc.
- **Round 5:** Ch 1, * 1 sc in next 2 sc, 2 sc in next sc, repeat from * around, sl st in 1 sc (24 sc).
- **Round 6:** Ch 1, * 1 sc in next 3 sc, 2 sc in next sc, repeat from * around, sl st in 1 sc (30 sc).

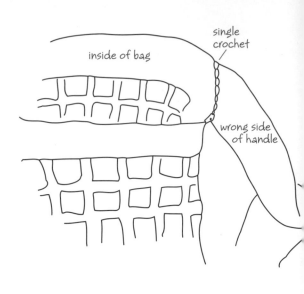

inside of bag

single crochet

wrong side of handle

- **Round 7:** Ch 1, * 1 sc in next 4 sc, 2 sc in next sc, repeat from * around, sl st in 1 sc (36 sc).
- **Round 8:** Ch 1, 1 sc in each sc around, sl st in 1st sc.
- **Round 9:** Ch 1, * 1 sc in next 5 sc, 2 sc in next sc, repeat from * around, sl st in 1 sc (42 sc).
- **Round 10:** Ch 1, * 1 sc in next 6 sc, 2 sc in next sc, repeat from * around, sl st in 1 sc (48 sc).
- **Round 11:** Ch 1, * 1 sc in next 7 sc, 2 sc in next sc, repeat from * around, sl st in 1 sc (54 sc).
- **Round 12:** Ch 1, 1 sc in each sc around, sl st in 1st sc.
- **Round 13:** Ch 1, * 1 sc in next 8 sc, 2 sc in next sc, repeat from * around, sl st in 1 sc (60 sc).
- **Round 14:** Ch 1, * 1 sc in next 9 sc, 2 sc in next sc, repeat from * around, sl st in 1 sc (66 sc).
- **Round 15:** Ch 1, 2 sc in next sc, 30 sc, 2 sc in next sc, sc to end of round, sl st in 1 st sc (68 sc).

Side

- Begin double-crochet mesh stitch in rounds.
  - **Round 16:** Ch 5, * skip 2 stitches, dc in next stitch, ch 2, repeat from * around, end with slip stitch in 3rd chain of beginning chain.
- Repeat round 16 15 more times.
  - **Round 32:** Ch 3, * 2 dc in ch 2 space, 1 dc in next dc, repeat from * around, join with slip stitch in top of ch 3.
- Repeat round 32 once more.

- **Round 34:** Ch 1, sc in each stitch around, end yarn.

Handle

- With right side of bag facing, attach yarn to top and sc across 10 sc, ch 1, turn.
- **Row 1:** Sc across 10 sc, ch 1, turn.
- Repeat row 1 until handle is 24 in. (61cm) or desired length.

TIP: A too-short handle will make the bag harder to use. Test the length before attaching it permanently.

- Holding right side of handle to right side of bag, make a sc seam through both fabrics to attach handle to other side of bag. End off and work all ends in.

TIP: Be sure to work through both loops on the handle and bag top for a sturdy join.

Finishing

- Press bottom and handle if necessary.
- Make a 3 in. (7.6cm) tassel and attach to center bottom.
- If desired, cut a 6 in. (15cm) diameter circle from foam board or cardboard and insert to stiffen base.

Creative Options

✳ Today's hot, eco-friendly yarns are just the ticket for these bags. Make several bags for intensive shopping sprees.

✳ Make the bag in a friend's favorite color, fill it with bath supplies or other favorite goodies, and you've got the perfect gift.

✳ Stripes are a bold and eye-catching addition. To make them, alternate color rounds while working the mesh stitch body of the bag.

Casual Cushion

This decorative and useful cushion fits right into your casual lifestyle. It's easy to make and large enough to lounge on. The interesting texture will have everyone asking, "Where did you get that?"

Finished Size:
Approximately 18 in. (46cm) square.

Techniques and Skills Used:
Chain stitch (p. 17), **single crochet** (p. 18), **reverse single crochet** (p. 19), **triple crochet** (p. 21)

Project Gauge:
14 stitches/3¾ in. (9.5cm) over pattern stitch.
3 rows/1½ in. (3.8cm) over pattern stitch

Note: Take time to check the gauge for this project to make sure your finished pillow fits the insert.

Materials:
- **Yarn:** 100% cotton, worsted-weight yarn, 710 yd. (649m) per skein, 1 skein per pillow
- **Crochet hook:** size J (5.5mm) or size needed for gauge
- **Pillow form:** 18 in. (46cm) square
- **Spray starch (optional)**
- **Tapestry or yarn needle**
- **Tape measure**
- **Scissors**

Note: The sample used nearly all the yarn in one large skein. You may want to purchase extra yarn to be sure you have enough and to make more cushions.

Finishing:
Single crochet seam (p. 26), **reverse single crochet** (p. 19)

Note: Two stitches of varying heights are used together for a strongly textured stitch. The pillow pieces are worked flat with no shaping. The cushion is finished by stitching the front and back together with single crochet and decorative reverse single crochet.

Pattern Stitch:
The pattern stitch is worked over a multiple of 2 stitches.
- Ch 15.
- **Row 1:** Sc in 2nd ch and in each ch across, ch 1 (counts as last sc throughout), turn.
- **Row 2:** Sc in first sc, * tc into next sc, sc in next sc, repeat from * across, end with sc in last 2 sc, ch 1 turn.
- **Row 3:** Sc in first two stitches, * tc into next sc, sc in next tc, repeat from * across, end with sc in last sc, ch 1 turn.
- Repeat rows 2 and 3 for pattern.
Swatch is 3¾ in. (9.5cm) wide.

Note: The first few rows will curl as you work. Don't worry; it flattens when finished. Push the triple crochet "bumps" to the front as you work.

TIP: You are simply alternating single crochet and triple crochet on alternate rows: Work single crochet on top of triple crochet and triple crochet on top of single crochet. Take your time getting used to this stitch pattern. It's not hard—it just takes practice.

YARN AND SUBSTITUTION INFORMATION

The yarn chosen for this project is a moderately heavy 100% cotton yarn that is slightly soft. Yarn label information suggests using size 7 (4.5mm) knitting needles or size G (4mm) crochet hook. The actual stitch gauge is not listed. It is a moderately twisted yarn and has a matte surface.

Other good choices would be organic cotton yarns or another natural fiber, such as linen or cotton blends. Acrylic yarns and blends in worsted weight would also work well for this project. The strong stitch pattern is complemented with a sturdy and durable yarn.

CUSHION

· Ch 62.

TIP: The starting chain should measure 17½–18 in. (44–46cm). If not, switch to a larger hook for the foundation, and then resume the stitch pattern with the smaller hook.

· **Row 1:** Sc in 2nd ch and in each ch across, ch 1, turn.
· **Row 2:** Sc in first sc, * trc into next sc, sc in next sc, repeat from * across, end with sc in last 2 sc, ch 1 turn.
· **Row 3:** Sc in first two stitches, * tc into next sc, sc in next tc, repeat from * across, end with sc in last sc, ch 1 turn.
· Repeat rows 2 and 3 until piece measures 17½ in. (44cm).
· Work 1 row of sc, end off and work ends in.
· Make 2.

Finishing

· Press well from wrong side; starch lightly, if desired.

TIP: Press on a padded surface such as a thick towel to avoid crushing the texture.

· Holding pieces wrong-sides together, attach yarn at corner, chain 1 and single crochet through both thicknesses.
· Work around three sides, insert pillow form, and continue across last side to close, slip stitch in beginning chain.

TIP: Work 3 stitches in each corner to prevent curling.

· Ch 1, work reverse single crochet around for decorative edge, end yarn and work ends in.

Creative Options

* Embellish your cushions with fringed edges and tasseled corners.

* Vary the size to make a set. To make a 14-in. (36cm) square pillow, chain 50 to start. For a 12-in. (30cm) pillow, chain 44 and begin the stitch pattern.

* This stitch pattern is interesting in both stripes and variegated yarns. Alternate three or five color stripes, or choose a contrasting variegated yarn. The difference in stitch height in each row accents the color changes.

Not Your Granny's Rug

This modern rug is at home with any décor. It is a modular rug based on the classic granny square. Granny squares are great for using up small amounts of yarn, and each individual motif is small and portable for on-the-go crocheting.

Finished Size:
About 45 x 26 in. (1.1m x 66cm), not including fringe

Techniques and Skills Used:
Chain stitch (p. 17), **slip stitch** (p. 18), **half-double crochet** (p. 19), **double crochet** (p. 20)

Finishing:
Crochet border, fringe (p. 28)

Note: Individual squares are crocheted together to make the finished rug.

Project Gauge:
1 unit/4 in. (10cm) square

Note: If your squares are significantly smaller or larger, the project will not be the stated size. Adjust hook size for correct gauge.

Materials:
• **Yarn:** 50% llama, 50% wool, heavy worsted-weight yarn, 127 yd. (116m) per skein, in ivory, 5 skeins; blue, 2 skeins; and yellow, 2 skeins
• **Crochet hook:** size J (6mm) or size needed for gauge
• **Tapestry or yarn needle**
• **Tape measure**
• **Scissors**

Note: Generous fringe, as shown on the sample, will take nearly one full skein (included in yarn amounts given).

Pattern Stitch:
Make one granny square:
• Ch 4, join with slip stitch to form ring.
• **Round 1:** Ch 5 (counts as 1 dc and ch 2 throughout), * 3 dc in ring, ch 2, repeat from * two times, 2 dc in ring, slip stitch to 3rd chain of beginning chain.
• **Round 2:** Ch 5, 3 dc in same space, * ch 1, skip 3 dc, (3 dc, ch 2, 3 dc) into next space, repeat from * twice, ch 1, skip 3 stitches, 2 dc into same space as beginning chain, slip stitch to 3rd chain of beginning chain.
• **Round 3:** Ch 5, 3 dc in same space, * ch 1, skip 3 dc, 3 dc into next space, 1 ch, skip 3 dc, (3 dc, ch 2, 3 dc) into next space (corner made), repeat from * twice, ch 1, skip 3 dc, 3 dc in next space, ch 1, skip 3 stitches, 2 dc into same space as beginning chain, slip stitch to 3rd chain of beginning chain.

• End yarn and work ends in.
Granny square measures 4 in. (10cm) square.

Note: Work over the beginning tail when working into the ring to save time working ends in.

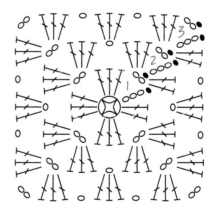

YARN AND SUBSTITUTION INFORMATION

The yarn chosen for this project is a substantial, heavy worsted-weight blend of wool and llama fiber. Yarn label information suggests a knit gauge of 16 stitches to 4 in. (10cm) on size 9 (5.5mm) knitting needles. It is a single-ply yarn of a uniform diameter. The strand is hairy with soft fibers.

Choose a heavyweight yarn with a substantial feel and very little loft. Wool and wool blends, as well as cotton and cotton blends, will make a long-wearing and comfortable rug. Choose synthetics with care, as they can stain carpet and may be slippery on smooth floors. Furry and textured yarns may be difficult to use and will obscure the granny square stitch pattern.

RUG
• Make 60 total squares as follows, using the gauge swatch instructions:
28 ivory
18 blue
14 yellow
• Weave all ends in.

Finishing

• With main color and holding squares right-side together, single crochet through both units. Attach squares into 10-unit strips according to diagram. Attach strips together on long edges.

TIP: Lay the squares out before assembly to check placement.

• With right side facing, attach main color along one long edge.
• **Round 1:** Ch 2, work half-double crochet in each stitch around, making 3 stitches in each corner, join to beginning chain with slip stitch, ch 1.
• **Round 2:** Sc in each stitch through back loop only, making 3 stitches in each corner, join with slip stitch. End yarn and work ends in.
• With main color, attach 5 in. (13cm) fringe to ends.

Creative Options

✻ Try different color schemes with more or fewer colors. Make every square a different color for a rainbow rug, or use closely related colors for a sophisticated look.

✻ Assemble the squares in different patterns. Lay them out to assess the design before crocheting them together.

✻ Make coordinating pillows by attaching 16 squares to make one pillow cover. Make a larger, smaller, skinnier, or fatter piece as a throw or blanket.

✻ Be adventurous—make a huge granny square! Repeat round three, adding ch 1, 3 dc blocks across the sides to keep in the pattern. The corners are as noted.

Why Back Loop Only?

Working through the back loop only lends a completely different look to the simple single and half-double crochet stitches. It forms a strong ridge that is decorative and emphasizes the border.

28 ivory
18 blue
14 yellow

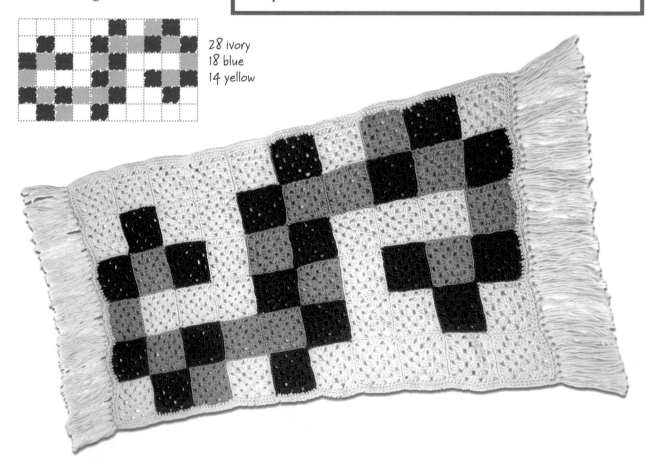

Get Organized Storage Baskets

Make a set of these handy containers to keep your stuff together, from paper clips to magazines. Simply made of single and half-double crochet, the variegated yarn adds color interest. These baskets are firm and sturdy. There is no shaping, and the sides are formed by picking up stitches around the base.

Finished Size:
Small: 3 x 4 x 1 in
(7.6 x 10 x 2.5cm)
Medium: 5 x 7½
x 1½ in. (13 x 19 x
3.8cm)
Large: 10 x 14 x
2 in. (25 x 36 x
5cm)

**Techniques and
Skills Used:
Chain stitch**
(p. 17), **slip stitch**
(p. 18), **single
crochet** *(p. 18)*,
**half-double
crochet** *(p. 19)*

**Finishing:
Stiffening and
shaping**

Materials:
- **Yarn:** 100% cotton, worsted-weight yarn,
  710 yd. (649m), 1 skein makes 3 baskets
- **Crochet hook:** size G (4mm) or size
  needed for gauge
- **Fabric stiffener or white glue**
- **Cardboard, three pieces:** small, 3 x 4 in.
  (7.6 x 10cm); medium, 5 x 7½ in. (13 x
  19cm); large, 10 x 14 in. (25 x 36cm)
- **Aluminum foil**
- **Tapestry or yarn needle**
- **Tape measure**
- **Yarn cutter**

*Note: There will be enough yarn left over to
make more baskets or other projects.*

Project Gauge:
8 hdc/2 in. (5cm)
7 rows in hdc/2½ in. (6.3cm)

*Note: If you want your containers to be a specific
size, be sure to work to gauge. If you don't mind
smaller or larger baskets, just be sure that the
gauge you obtain will make a nice, firm fabric.
If your gauge varies significantly, you may need
more or less yarn than specified.*

Pattern Stitch:
The pattern stitch is simply half-double crochet.
- Ch 17.
- **Row 1:** 1 hdc in 3rd ch from hook and each ch across, ch 2 turn
  (16 hdc).
- **Row 2:** 1 hdc in each stitch across, ch 2 turn.
- Repeat row 2 for 6 rows total.
Swatch measures 4 x 2½ in. (10 x 6.3cm).

YARN AND SUBSTITUTION INFORMATION

The yarn chosen for this project is
a moderately heavy, 100% cotton
yarn. Yarn label information
suggests 20 stitches to 4 in. (4cm)
on size 7 (4.5mm) needles. It is a
moderately twisted yarn and has a
matte surface.

Other good choices would be
any yarn that can be worked into
a firm fabric, including acrylics
and blends. Variegated colors lend
interest to the simple stitches, but
solid colors, especially in natural
tones, would look sophisticated.

Highly textured and furry yarns
are not suitable for this project

because the stiffening process
will obscure or mat the texture.
Avoid very soft yarns because they
may not produce a container with
enough structure to be functional.

SMALL BASKET

Make Base
- Ch 15.
- **Row 1:** 1 hdc in 3rd ch from
  hook and each ch across, ch 2
  turn (13 hdc).
- **Row 2:** 1 hdc in each stitch
  across, ch 2 turn.
- Repeat row 2 for 12 rows.
- End yarn and work in ends.

Make Sides
- **Round 1:** Attach yarn in
  middle of long side of base,
  ch 1, sc along edges—17 sc
  evenly spaced along long sides
  and 13 sc on short sides. Join
  to beginning chain 1 with slip
  stitch (60 sc).

TIP: Be sure that stitches are
only on edges, not in the corners
of the base. This will help keep
the corners square.

- **Round 2:** Ch 2, 1 hdc in each sc
  around, join with slip stitch in
  top of beginning chain.
- Work round 2 once more or
  until desired height. End off and
  work in ends.

MEDIUM BASKET

Make Base
- Ch 22.
- **Row 1:** 1 hdc in 3rd ch from
  hook and each ch across, ch 2
  turn (20 hdc).
- **Row 2:** 1 hdc in each stitch
  across, ch 2 turn.
- Repeat row 2 for 21 rows.
- Cut yarn and work ends in.

Make Sides

- **Round 1:** Attach yarn in middle of long side of base, ch 1, sc along edges—29 sc evenly spaced along long sides and 20 sc on short sides. Join to beginning chain 1 with slip stitch (98 sc).
- **Round 2:** Ch 2, 1 hdc in each sc around, join with slip stitch in top of beginning chain.
- Work round 2 three more times or until desired height. End off and work in ends.

LARGE BASKET

Make Base

- Ch 38.
- **Row 1:** 1 hdc in 3rd ch from hook and each ch across, ch 2 turn (36 hdc).
- **Row 2:** 1 hdc in each stitch across, ch 2 turn.
- Repeat row 2 for 36 rows.
- Break yarn and work ends in.

Make Sides

- **Round 1:** Attach yarn in middle of long side of base, ch 1, sc along edges—50 sc evenly spaced along long sides and 36 sc on short sides. Join to beginning ch 1 with slip stitch (172 sc).
- **Round 2:** Ch 2, 1 hdc in each sc around, join with slip stitch in top of beginning chain.
- Work round 2 seven more times or until desired height. End off and work in ends.

FINISHING

- Make base templates by cutting cardboard to fit inside of baskets.
- Check that cardboard templates fit inside basket bottoms tightly. Trim templates if necessary. Cover with aluminum foil to prevent the templates from sticking to the yarn.

Creative Options

* Work a row of reverse single crochet around the top for a more defined edge.

* Make a set of baskets in natural-colored linen or cotton. After stiffening, attach strands of raffia to the top with glue.

* Attach tassels or other embellishments to the sides and corners.

* Make the bases and sides with stripes.

- Wet the baskets with fabric stiffener. Wring out excess stiffener and insert base templates. Shape sides and corners while damp. Let dry completely. Remove cardboard templates.

TIP: Make homemade fabric stiffener from white household glue: Dilute white glue 50% with water and mix well.

A Custom Fit

Want a custom size? Make the base the width and length you want. Make the sides by working single crochet around the base in each stitch across the ending and beginning rows. Single crochet evenly along the rows with about four stitches in every three rows. Work single crochet rounds to the desired depth.

Lacy Café Curtains

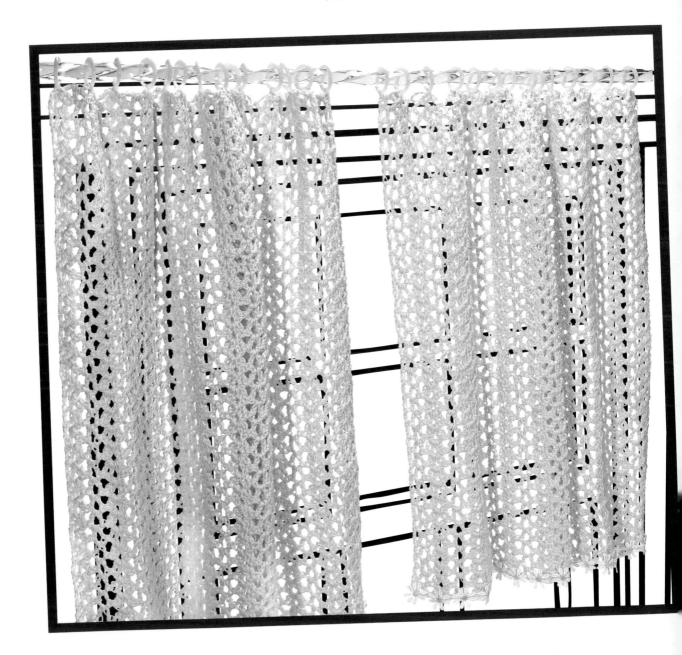

Make this dramatic and easy curtain for your kitchen or bath. The simple lace pattern is charming for any small window, and you can add embellishments to coordinate with your décor.

Finished Size:
About 22 x 20 in. (56 x 51cm) per curtain panel

Note: Smaller curtains are more effective and easier to make. Large expanses of hand-worked lace are impressive, but may not hang well and take far too long to finish.

Techniques and Skills Used:
Chain stitch (p. 17), **single crochet** (p. 18), **double crochet** (p. 20)

Project Gauge:
2 pattern repeats/4 in. (10cm)
8 pattern rows/4 in. (10cm)

Note: Gauge is not critical. The curtain only has to fit the window. Be sure that the gauge you obtain will make an attractive curtain fabric (not too stiff or too limp). If your gauge varies significantly, you may need more or less yarn than specified.

Finishing:
Attaching motifs

Materials:
- **Yarn:** 100% cotton sport-weight yarn, 100 yd. (91m) per ball, 7 balls for 2 curtain panels
- **Crochet hook:** size G (4mm) or size needed for gauge
- **Daisy trim:** 4 ft. (1.2m)
- **Plastic (cabone) rings:** 1⅛ in. (28mm), 28 rings
- **Spray starch (optional)**
- **Sewing needle and matching thread**
- **Tapestry or yarn needle**
- **Tape measure**
- **Scissors**

Note: The sample project used all the stated yarn. Purchase extra to be sure you have enough and to adjust the length.

Pattern Stitch:

The pattern stitch is worked over a multiple of 9 stitches plus 1 for starting chain.
- Ch 19.
- **Row 1:** 2 dc in 5th ch from hook, ch 1, 2 dc in same ch, * skip 3 ch, (dc, ch 2, dc) into next ch, skip 3 ch, (2 dc, ch 1, 2 dc) into next chain, repeat from * across, ending with (dc, ch 2, dc) in 3rd ch from end, dc in last ch, ch 3, turn.
- **Row 2:** (Dc, ch 2, dc) into first ch 2 space, * (2 dc, ch 1, 2 dc) into next ch 1 space, (dc, ch 2, dc) into next ch 2 space, repeat from * across, ending with dc in top of turning ch, ch 3, turn.
- **Row 3:** * (2 dc, ch 1, 2 dc) into next ch 1 space,

(dc, ch 2, dc) into next ch 2 space, repeat from * across, ending with dc in top of turning ch, ch 3, turn.
- Repeat rows 2 and 3 for pattern.
Swatch measures 4 in. (10cm) wide.

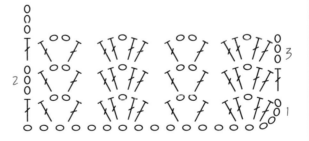

YARN AND SUBSTITUTION INFORMATION:

The yarn chosen for this project is a cabled cotton lightweight yarn. Yarn label information suggests a knit gauge of 17 stitches to 4 in. (10cm) on size 7 (4.5mm) knitting needles. It is a well-cabled yarn with a smooth, shiny surface.

Choose a similar lightweight or sport-weight yarn with a moderate to high amount of twist or a cable construction. Cotton or a cotton blend with linen, rayon, or even acrylic should give pleasing results.

To duplicate the look here, do not choose a much heavier or thicker yarn, as it may not hang attractively. Yarns with dull or fuzzy surfaces will not show the stitch pattern off as well as those with a smooth surface.

CURTAIN
- Ch 110.
- **Row 1:** 2 dc in 5th ch from hook, ch 1, 2 dc in same ch, * skip 3 ch, (dc, ch 2, dc) into next ch, skip 3 ch, (2 dc, ch 1, 2 dc) into next chain, repeat from * across, ending with (dc, ch 2, dc) in 3rd ch from end, dc in last ch, ch 3, turn.
- **Row 2:** (dc, ch 2, dc) into first ch 2 space, * (2 dc, ch 1, 2 dc) into next ch 1 space, (dc, ch 2, dc) into next ch 2 space, repeat from * across, ending with dc in top of turning ch, ch 3, turn.
- **Row 3:** * (2 dc, ch 1, 2 dc) into next ch 1 space, (dc, ch 2, dc)

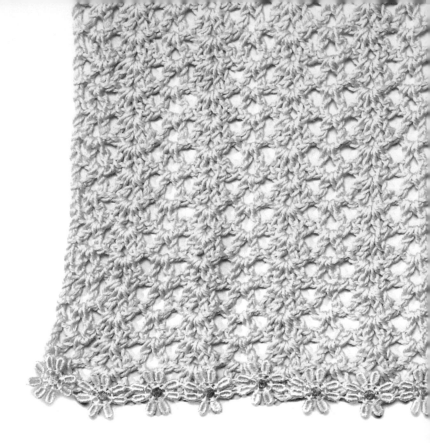

into next ch 2 space, repeat from * across, ending with dc in top of turning ch, ch 3, turn.

- Repeat rows 2 and 3 for until curtain measures 20 in. (51cm) or desired length.
- End yarn and work ends in.
- Make 2 or as many as needed to cover window.

Finishing

- Press panels well; lightly starch if desired.
- Using sewing needle and thread, sew rings to top of curtain. Sew trim to bottom.

TIP: The bottom of the curtain when hung is the last row worked. The top is the beginning chain.

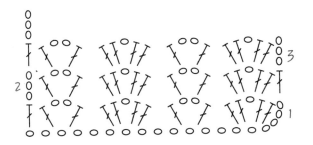

Creative Options

✱ Use clip rings instead of sew-on rings, or embellish the rings with glue-on trims.

✱ Try adding tassels, beaded or not, to the scallops at the bottom of the curtain.

✱ Attach additional trim motifs randomly across the curtain.

Table Runner & Place Mats

Colorful stripes and an easy stitch pattern combine to make a stunning table setting. The fabric looks complex, but it is easy to work. Make a set for yourself and as gifts for friends using eco-friendly natural fibers—the variations are endless.

Finished Size:
Runner: 14 x 32 in.
(36 x 81cm)
Place mats: 14 x
18 in. (36 x 46cm)

**Techniques and
Skills Used:**
Chain stitch (p. 17),
single crochet
(p. 18), **half-double
crochet** (p. 19),
double crochet
(p. 20)

Materials:
• **Yarn:** 100% Peruvian cotton, worsted-
  weight yarn, 82 yd. (75m) per skein
  1 table runner: turquoise (color A), 3
  skeins; sea green (color B), 2 skeins; light
  yellow (color C), 2 skeins
  1 place mat: turquoise, 2 skeins; sea
  green, 1 skein; light yellow, 1 skein
• **Crochet hook:** size J (6mm) or size
  needed for gauge
• **Spray starch (optional)**
• **Tapestry or yarn needle**
• **Tape measure**
• **Scissors**

*Note: If you make multiple place mats, you
may require fewer skeins per place mat.*

Finishing:
Fringe (p. 28)

*Note: Two different-
sized stitches combine
to make a textured
fabric. There is no
shaping, and the
edges are finished
with single crochet.*

Project Gauge:
12 stitches/4 in. (10cm) over pattern.

*Note: If you want your project to be the
specified size, be sure to work to gauge. If you
don't mind smaller or larger projects, just
be sure that the gauge you obtain makes a
suitable fabric.*

Pattern Stitch:
• Ch 13.
• **Row 1:** Sc in 2nd chain from hook and each ch across, ch 3,
  turn (12 sc stitches).
• **Row 2:** Skip 1st sc, * sc in next sc, dc in next sc, repeat from *
  across, sc in last sc, ch 3 turn.
• **Row 3:** * Sc in next dc, dc in next sc, repeat from * across, sc in
  turning ch 3, ch 3, turn.
• Repeat row 3 for pattern.
Swatch measures 4 in. (10cm) wide.

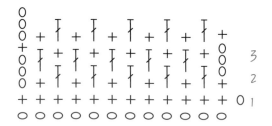

YARN AND SUBSTITUTION INFORMATION

These table accessories are made
of worsted-weight, 100% Peruvian
cotton yarn. Label information
suggests 4.5 stitches to 1 in.
(2.5cm) with size 7 (4.5mm)
knitting needles. The yarn is soft
and moderately fuzzy. The strand
is composed of cotton fibers with
very little twist wrapped with a
smaller, firmer strand that gives a
wavy surface texture.

When choosing a different yarn,
select yarns that can be washed
easily. The cotton chosen for the
project is absorbent, which makes
the mat easier and more pleasant
to use. Linen is a classic table
fiber and would be hard-wearing
and practical.

To duplicate the look and feel
of the model, choose a yarn that
is soft and not shiny. Shiny,
textured, or bulky yarns may
interfere with the stitch and stripe
patterns. These yarns are also not
practical for the table because fuzz
and fibers can get in your food. If
you choose a significantly heavier
weight yarn, the runner and mats
will be much thicker and larger,

Stitch Names

This pattern is called
griddle stitch in some stitch
dictionaries. Many stitch
patterns have colorful or
descriptive names. Some
stitches can have many
different names, so be sure
to check the diagrams or
instructions for a specific
stitch.

so make a swatch first to test your choice. Yarn requirements can vary significantly with a different weight of yarn.

RUNNER

- With turquoise (color A), ch 44.
- **Row 1:** Sc in 2nd chain from hook and each ch across, ch 3, turn (43 sc stitches). Drop A, attach sea green (color B).
- **Row 2:** Skip 1st sc, * sc in next sc, dc in next sc, repeat from * across, sc in last sc, drop B, attach light yellow (color C), ch 3 turn.
- **Row 3:** * Sc in next dc, dc in next sc, repeat from * across, sc in turning ch 3, drop C, pick up A, ch 3, turn.
- Repeat row 3 for stitch pattern, and continue changing colors in sequence. Work until piece measures about 32 in. (81cm) long, ending with color C.
- **Last Row:** Pick up A, work 1 hdc in each stitch across, end all yarns. Work all ends in.

TIP: Don't cut the yarns as you change colors. Instead, carry them along the sides of the piece, being sure not to pull tight when picking them up again. These yarn floats will be covered later by the edging. Stripes made with uneven numbers of rows allow you to carry them along.

PLACE MATS

- Work as for runner until piece measures approximately 18 in. (46cm). End as for runner.
- Make 4 mats.

FINISHING

- With A and right side facing, attach yarn to corner of long edge, work sc evenly spaced

along edge. Repeat along other side.
- Press carefully from the wrong side, and starch lightly if desired for more body. Pressing from the front will flatten the stitch texture.

TIP: Long, thin crocheted items often benefit from pressing; it helps to make the shape more regular and straight.

TIP: Spray starch will add stain resistance as well as stiffness.

- Fringe the ends with 5-in. (13cm) fringe.

TIP: Make fringe longer than you think you need—it can always be trimmed shorter. Too-short fringe looks skimpy.

Creative Options

* Instead of stripes, use variegated yarn. Make a test swatch to make sure you like the effect.
* Make the stripes with five colors. Carry the unused yarns up the sides as noted.
* Use a solid neutral yarn trimmed with wooden beads or seashells for a natural look.
* Trim the ends with tassels instead of fringe.

Felted Basket

Organize all your essentials with this felted basket. The unique shape is great for decorative display.

Finished Size:
Pre-felting: About 14 in. (35cm) diameter and 10 in. (25cm) tall
Post-felting: About 10 in. (25cm) diameter and 5 in. (13cm) tall

Techniques and Skills Used:
Chain stitch *(p. 17)*, **slip stitch** *(p. 18)*, **half-double crochet** *(p. 19)*

Finishing:
Felting *(p. 28)*

Note: The basket bottom is worked flat with the sides picked up and worked in the round. The sides are shaped with increases to flare outward slightly. The basket is felted to finish.

Materials:
• **Yarn:** 100% merino wool, worsted-weight yarn, 216 yd. (198m) per skein, kettle-dyed variegated colors, 2 skeins
• **Crochet hook:** size K (6.5mm) or size needed for gauge
• **Tapestry or yarn needle**
• **Tape measure**
• **Scissors**

Project Gauge:
Pre-felting: 15 hdc/4½ in. (11cm), 9 rows/4 in. (10cm)
Post-felting: 15 hdc/3¾ in. (9.5cm), 9 rows/3¼ in. (8.2cm)

Note: Gauge is not critical and won't be exact. Felting is an imprecise art, so the finished size and shape may vary due to factors in the felting process.

Pattern Stitch:
The pattern stitch is half-double crochet.
• Ch 16.
• **Row 1:** Hdc in 3rd ch from hook and in each ch to end, ch 2, turn (15 hdc, including beginning ch 2).
• **Row 2:** Skip 1st hdc, hdc in each stitch across, ch 2, turn.
• Repeat row 2 for 9 rows total.
Swatch measures 4½ in. (11cm) wide and 4 in. (10cm) tall before felting; swatch measures 3¾ in. (9.5cm) wide and 3¼ in. (8.2cm) wide after felting.

YARN AND SUBSTITUTION INFORMATION

This handy basket is made of 100% merino wool. The yarn is worsted weight and soft with very little twist to the strand. Yarn label information suggests 4 to 5 stitches per 1 in. (2.5cm) with needles ranging from size 7–9 (4.5–5.5mm). The strand has a soft, fuzzy surface with no shine.

The only type of yarn that will produce a suitable finish is wool that has not been treated to be washable. Other yarns will not felt properly. Avoid yarns labeled "superwash."

The model project was worked in a strongly variegated hand-dyed yarn that felts for a multicolored effect. While the variegation adds interest to this project, a solid color would be equally attractive.

BASKET

Make Base
• Ch 29.
• **Row 1:** Hdc in 3rd ch from hook and in each ch to end, ch 2, turn (28 hdc).
• **Row 2:** Skip 1st hdc, hdc in each stitch across, ch 2, turn.
• Repeat row 2 for 20 rows total, or until piece measures 7 in. (18cm).

TIP: Mark beginning of rounds at corner of base.

Pick Up and Work Sides

- Ch 2 (counts as first stitch picked up), pick up 28 stitches along each free edge of base (112 stitches around).
- Join with sl st in beginning ch 2 and start working in joined rounds.
- **Round 1:** Ch 2, hdc in each stitch around, join with sl st in beginning ch 2.
- **Rounds 2–5:** Repeat round 1.
- **Round 6:** Ch 2, * 2 hdc in next stitch, 9 hdc, repeat from *, join with sl st in beginning ch 2 (124 stitches, including beginning ch 2).
- **Rounds 7–11:** Repeat round 1.
- **Round 12:** Ch 2, * 2 hdc in next stitch, 10 hdc, repeat from *, join with sl st in beginning ch 2 (136 stitches, including beginning ch 2).
- **Rounds 13–17:** Repeat round 1.
- **Round 18:** Ch 2, * 2 hdc in next stitch, 11 hdc, repeat from *, join with sl st in beginning ch 2 (148 stitches, including beginning ch 2).
- **Rounds 19–23:** Repeat round 1.
- **Round 24:** Ch 2, * 2 hdc in next stitch, 12 hdc, repeat from *, join with sl st in beginning ch 2 (160 stitches, including beginning ch 2).

Make Handles

TIP: Start this round at the beginning of the rounds corresponding to the corner of the square base.

- **Round 25:** Ch 2, hdc in next 14 stitches, ch 20, skip 12 hdc on body of bag, hdc in next 68 stitches, ch 20, skip 12 hdc on body of bag, hdc in next 54 stitches, join with sl st in beginning ch 2.

- **Round 26:** Ch 2, work hdc in hdc and chains (continue to work in rounds on 176 stitches) around, join with sl st in beginning ch 2.
- **Rounds 27 and 28:** Repeat round 26.
- End yarn and work ends in.

Felting

- Felt (see p. 28).

Creative Options

❋ Make a festive striped basket. Work rows of two or more colors, and invent your own color scheme.

❋ Use leftover yarns at random for a scrap basket. Just be sure all of the yarn will felt.

❋ Sew on embellishments, such as silk flowers, buttons, and beads.

Projects

Great Gifts

Kitty Cushion & Toy
Beginner Baby Blanket
Cute Crochet Critters
Felted Oven Mitts
Felted Hook Book

Kitty Cushion & Toy

This project is especially for kitty! A fun jingle toy with optional catnip and a soft cushy pillow—cat sized—makes a perfect gift for your furry friend. The crocheted cover over a purchased pillow form is removable for washing.

Finished Size:
Cushion: 14 in. (36cm) square
Toy: 24 in. (61cm) long, including tassel

Techniques and Skills Used:
Chain stitch *(p. 17)*, **slip stitch** *(p. 18)*, **single crochet** *(p. 18)*, **double crochet** *(p. 20)*

Project Gauge:
20 st/4½ in. (11cm)
3 rows/1 in. (2.5cm)

Materials:
- **Yarn:** 80% acrylic, 20% wool, worsted-weight yarn, 197 yd. (180m) per skein, 3 skeins
- **Crochet hook:** size G (4mm) or size needed for gauge
- **Pillow form:** 14 in. (36cm) square
- **Jingle bell:** 16mm
- **Catnip** (optional)
- **Sewing needle and thread**
- **Tapestry or yarn needle**
- **Tape measure**
- **Scissors**

Finishing:
Seaming by working two thicknesses together, attach tassels

Note: Single-crochet and double-crochet stitches are alternated to create a textured fabric cover that is worked flat with no shaping. The pillow cover is finished by working single crochet through front and back layers. The toy is a double-crochet tube worked in rounds.

Pattern Stitch:
The pattern stitch is a multiple of two stitches.
- Ch 22.
- **Row 1:** * 1 sc in fourth chain from hook, 1 dc in next ch, repeat from * across, ending 1 sc into last ch, ch 3, turn.
- **Row 2:** * 1 sc into next dc, 1 dc into next sc, repeat from * across, ending 1 sc in top of ch 3, ch 3, turn.
- Repeat row 2 for pattern.
Swatch measures 4½ in. (11cm) wide.

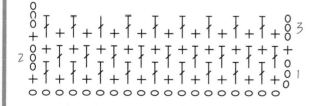

YARN AND SUBSTITUTION INFORMATION

The yarn chosen for this project is a worsted-weight, 80% acrylic, 20% wool blend. Yarn label information suggests 13.2 single crochet stitches or 18 stockinette stitches to 4 in. (10cm) with a size J (5.5mm) hook or size 8 (5mm) knitting needles. This yarn is a basic, well-twisted yarn.

The yarn you choose should be sturdy with a tightly twisted strand. More twist in the strand lends some strength to the finished project to help it withstand use and snags. Above all, the yarn should be machine washable and dryable. Superwash wools, blends, or even synthetics in plain worsted weight would make great choices. Choose bright colors and variegated yarns to add interest.

No matter how tempting, stay away from highly textured and furry yarns. They can snag and catch in your pets' claws. Also they are not usually made for hard use and may show wear quickly.

CUSHION

- Ch 62.
- **Row 1:** * 1 sc in 4th chain from hook, 1 dc in next ch, repeat from * across, ending 1 sc into last ch, ch 3, turn.
- **Row 2:** * 1 sc into next dc, 1 dc into next sc, repeat from * across, ending 1 sc in top of ch 3, ch 3, turn.

- Repeat row 2 until piece measures 32 in. (81cm).
- Cut yarn and work ends in.

TOY

- **Round 1:** Ch 3 (counts as 1st dc), 9 dc in 3rd chain from hook, slip stitch to top of beginning chain 3 (10 dc).

TIP: Joining to the beginning chain allows you to work the tube in separate rounds on 10 stitches. Be sure to keep an eye on your stitch count as you go.

- **Round 2:** Ch 3, dc in each stitch around, slip stitch to top of beginning ch 3.
- Repeat round 2 until tube measures 22 in. (56cm). Cut yarn, leaving 8 in. (20cm) tail.
- Insert bell.
- Insert small cloth packet of catnip before closing the toy to entice kitty even more.
- Thread tail into yarn needle and stitch around opening, draw

tight to close. Secure yarn and work ends in.

FINISHING

Cushion:

- With right sides out, fold rectangle with 4 in. (10cm) overlap in middle.
- Pin the edges closed with long pins with large heads.
- With pillow top facing, attach yarn to corner at fold, chain 1. Single crochet evenly along open edges, catching all thicknesses. Repeat for other side. Insert pillow form through opening.

TIP: Commercial pillow forms are firm and full of stuffing. To make a comfortable cat cushion, remove some stuffing. Cut a slit in the cover and remove the filling to make a flatter pillow. Hand-sew the opening closed with sewing needle and thread.

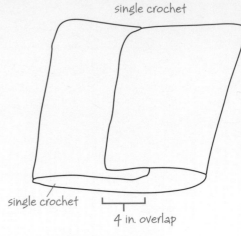

single crochet

single crochet

4 in. overlap

Cushion Assembly

TIP: Using single crochet to join the pillow thicknesses makes an attractive edge without bulky seam allowances.

- Make four 3-in. (7.6cm) tassels. Attach one to each corner.

Toy

- Tie a knot at one end to keep bell in place.
- Make one 3-in. (7.6cm) tassel and attach to other end.

Creative Options

✳ This stitch pattern looks interesting in different color stripes. For ideas, see the "Table Runner & Place Mats," p. 71, for the same stitch pattern in stripes.

✳ These cushions aren't just for pets. Make a few for your sofa or bed in coordinating colors. Choose from a wide variety of yarns in different sizes and colors.

✳ This toy has been cat-tested and found to be fun! Some cats might like it better with more knots tied along the length.

Beginner Baby Blanket

This small blanket is a wonderful welcome for a cradle or bassinet. Make the larger blanket for a crib as a soft and cuddly gift. The lace pattern is simple but stunning, a look any new parent will love.

Finished Size:
Small: 21 x 25 in. (53 x 63cm)
Large: 30 x 36 in. (76 x 91cm)

Techniques and Skills Used:
Chain stitch *(p. 17)*, **double crochet**
(p. 20)

Finishing:
None required

Note: Two basic stitches are used to make a shell lace pattern. Once established, the stitch pattern is formed in one row and there is no shaping and minimal finishing.

Materials:
- **Yarn:** 100% acrylic, worsted-weight yarn, 166 yd. (152m) per skein, 3 (5) skeins
- **Crochet hook:** size J (5.5mm) or size needed for gauge
- **Ribbon rose individual flower trims**
- **Sewing needle and matching thread**
- **Tapestry or yarn needle**
- **Tape measure**
- **Scissors**

Project Gauge:
2 pattern repeats/5 in. (13cm) over pattern stitch
5 rows/3 in. (7.6cm) over pattern stitch

Note: Gauge is not critical; as long as the blanket is large enough to use in the stroller or crib, it will be fine. Be sure that the gauge you obtain will make an attractive blanket that's not too stiff or floppy.

Pattern Stitch:
The pattern stitch is worked over a multiple of 8 stitches plus 3 with 3 additional dc at each edge.
- Ch 25.
- **Row 1:** Dc in 4th ch and in each ch across, ch 3 (counts as last dc throughout), turn.
- **Row 2:** 1 dc into each of next 2 dc, 1 ch, skip 1 dc, 1 dc into next dc, * skip 2 dc, 5 dc in next dc, skip 2 dc, 1 dc into next dc, 1 ch, skip 1 dc, 1 dc into next dc, rep from * to end, dc in last 2 dc, ch 3, turn.
- **Row 3:** 1 dc into each of next 2 dc, 1 ch, skip ch sp, 1 dc into next dc, * skip 2 dc, 5 dc in next dc, skip 2 dc, 1 dc into next dc, 1 ch, skip ch sp, 1 dc into next dc, rep from * to end, dc in last 2 dc, ch 3, turn.
- Repeat row 3 four more times, repeat row 1 one time, end off. Swatch is 6 in. (15cm) wide and 5 in. (13cm) long.

YARN AND SUBSTITUTION INFORMATION

The yarn chosen for this project is a soft, worsted-weight acrylic yarn. Yarn label information suggests a knit gauge of 18 stitches to 4 in. (10cm) on size 8 (5mm) knitting needles, as well as a size H (5mm) crochet hook. It is a well-twisted yarn with a smooth, shiny surface.

Choose your yarn carefully when making items for a baby. No matter how lovely and soft they are, stay away from yarns that fuzz (like angora and mohair), as the loose fibers can find their way into the baby's eyes and mouth. Ease of care is important to the baby's parents, so stick with machine-washable and dryable yarns that will hold up well to frequent laundering.

Acrylic yarns are wonderful due to their ease of maintenance and sturdy construction. Washable cottons and wools are great choices as well. To make this blanket, pick a similar worsted-weight yarn with a smooth surface. If you choose a yarn that is lighter than worsted weight, the blanket will be smaller and the yarn requirements may differ. A heavyweight yarn is not recommended, as the blanket will be large and heavy, and the lace pattern may not be very attractive.

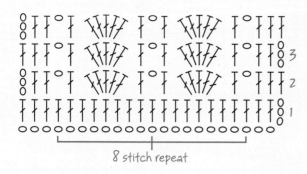

8 stitch repeat

BLANKET

Instructions for larger size are in parentheses.

- Ch 89 (105).
- **Row 1:** Dc in 4th ch and in each ch across, ch 3 (counts as last dc throughout), turn.
- **Row 2:** 1 dc into each of next 2 dc, 1 ch, skip 1 dc, 1 dc into next dc, * skip 2 dc, 5 dc in next dc, skip 2 dc, 1 dc into next dc, 1 ch, skip 1 dc, 1 dc into next dc, rep from * to end, dc in last 2 dc, ch 3, turn.
- **Row 3:** 1 dc into each of next 2 dc, 1 ch, skip ch sp, 1 dc into next dc, * skip 2 dc, 5 dc in next dc, skip 2 dc, 1 dc into next dc, 1 ch, skip ch sp, 1 dc into next dc, rep from * to end, dc in last 2 dc, ch 3, turn.
- Repeat row three 39 (59) more times for a total of 41 (61) pattern rows.
- Repeat row 1 once more, end off, and work all ends in.

TIP: Make the blanket any size you like by starting with a longer foundation chain and working to the desired length. To determine the number of chain stitches, start with a number divisible by 8 and add 9 edge stitches. For example 112 is divisible by eight; add 9 stitches for a total of 121 chains for a wider blanket.

Finishing

- Block if required.
- Using sewing thread and needle, attach one ribbon rosette at center of shells along top and bottom of blanket.

Safety Note

For young children and babies, do not attach small items to the blanket because they may be a choking hazard. The sample shown is only suitable for an older child due to the small ribbon roses. Any trims applied to a child or baby's item must be attached securely.

Creative Options

* Don't limit yourself to soft pastel colors. Jazz up baby's crib or stroller with a bright, cheerful color.

* Use a softly variegated yarn for more color interest. Choose a yarn that only has a few different colors so the blanket doesn't look too busy.

* Work a border of contrasting single-crochet stitches around the entire blanket. Work three stitches in each corner so the edging lies flat. Use white around soft colors and black around a bright color to really make the blanket pop.

* Make one for yourself! Use a heavy cotton or a fluffy mohair yarn to make a throw for your living room.

Cute Crochet Critters

These little critters are adorable. Crochet one for yourself, or give a personalized critter as a special gift. These are great toys for tots or pets.

Finished Size:
4–6 in. (10–15cm) tall

Techniques and Skills Used: Chain stitch *(p. 17)*, **slip stitch** *(p. 18)*, **single crochet** *(p. 18)*

Finishing: Seaming *(p. 26)*, **attaching parts**

Note: The toy is worked in spiral rounds, with some parts worked flat. Parts and embellishments are stuffed and then sewn.

Materials:
- **Yarn:** worsted-weight yarn, 50 yd. (46m) per critter; assorted small amounts (1 yd./91cm) in different colors for features and parts
- **Crochet hook:** size G (4mm) or size needed for gauge
- **Polyester fiberfill**
- **Safety or animal eyes:** 12mm
- **Buttons:** approximately ½ in. (12mm) for eyes
- **Embroidery needle and floss in colors to suit your design**
- **Tapestry or yarn needle**
- **Tape measure**
- **Scissors**

Project Gauge:
About 6–8 sc/2 in. (5cm)

Note: Gauge is not important, but the smaller the yarn and gauge, the smaller the toy.

Pattern Stitch:

The pattern stitch is simply single crochet worked in rounds. Do not count the joining slip stitch as a stitch, and do not work into it on subsequent rows.
- Ch 3.
- **Round 1:** 5 sc in 3rd ch from hook, sl st in top of beg ch.
- **Round 2:** Ch 1, 2 sc in each stitch around, sl st in 1st sc (12 sc).
- **Round 3:** Ch 1, * sc in 1st sc, 2sc in next sc, repeat from * around, sl st in 1st sc (18 sc).
- **Round 4:** Ch 1, 1 sc in each sc around, sl st in 1st sc, end off.
Swatch measures 2 in. (5cm) across.

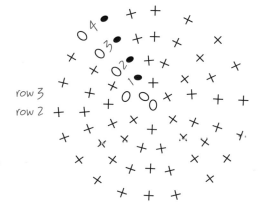

Marking Rounds

Mark the beginning of a round to start working spiral rounds. To mark rounds easily, use a long, contrasting-color smooth yarn. Weave the yarn back and forth up the rounds as you work. When you're finished, just pull out the yarn.

YARN AND SUBSTITUTION INFORMATION

The yarns chosen for this project are a mix of worsted-weight yarns in a variety of fibers. Yarn label information suggests knitting gauges ranging from 16–20 stitches to 4 in. (10cm) with size 7–8 (4.5–5mm) knitting needles and a size G (4mm) crochet hook. The characteristics of the yarns vary somewhat, but they are generally smooth yarns with some cotton content.

Any yarn that can be worked into a firm fabric, including acrylic and blends, would be fine. Variegated self-striping yarns lend interest to the simple stitches, but solid colors, especially bright ones, are a fun touch.

If you would like to substitute other yarns, feel free. The finished size of the critter is not as important as its personality. Color and texture give the toy its distinctive qualities, so choose what speaks to you. This time, leftovers are fine! Use up little bits and pieces of yarn from other projects and odd balls.

CRITTER BODY

- Ch 3.
- **Round 1:** 5 sc in 3rd ch from hook, sl st in top of beg ch.
- **Round 2:** Ch 1, 2 sc in each stitch around (12 sc).
- **Round 3:** * Sc in next sc, 2sc in next sc, repeat from * around (18 sc).
- **Round 4:** 1 sc in each sc around.
- **Round 5:** * 1 sc in next 2 sc, 2 sc in next sc, repeat from * around (24 sc).
- **Round 6:** 1 sc in each sc around.

- **Round 7:** * 1 sc in next 3 sc, 2 sc in next sc, repeat from * around (30 sc).
- **Round 8:** * 1 sc in next 4 sc, 2 sc in next sc, repeat from * around (36 sc).
- **Round 9:** 1 sc in each sc around, sl st in 1st sc.
- **Round 10:** * 1 sc in next 5 sc, 2 sc in next sc, repeat from * around (42 sc).
- Work even on 42 stitches for 4 rounds.

Begin Decrease Rounds

- **Round 15:** * 1 sc in next 5 sc, 2 sctog, repeat from * around (36 sc).
- **Round 16:** 1 sc in each sc around, sl st in 1st sc.
- **Round 17:** * 1 sc in next 4 sc, 2 sctog, repeat from * around (30 sc).
- **Round 18:** * 1 sc in next 3 sc, 2 sctog, repeat from * around (24 sc).
- **Round 19:** * 1 sc in next 2 sc, 2 sctog, repeat from * around (18 sc).
- **Round 20:** 1 sc in each sc around, sl st in 1st sc.
- Stuff body firmly.

TIP: If using safety eyes, insert and attach them before stuffing the body.

- **Round 21:** * 1 sc in next, 2 sctog, repeat from * around (12 sc).
- **Round 22:** * 1 sc in next, 2 sctog, repeat from * around (6 sc).
- Leaving 8 in. (20cm) tail, cut yarn.
- Thread tapestry needle with tail and weave around opening, tightening to close. Work end in.

Feet
Make 2.
- Ch 3.
- **Row 1:** 2 sc in 3rd chain from hook, ch 1, turn.
- **Row 2:** 2 sc in first sc, sc in next sc, 2 sc in beginning chain, ch 1, turn (5 sc).
- **Row 3:** 2 sc in first sc, sc in next 3 sc, 2 sc in last sc, ch 1, turn (7 sc).
- **Rows 4–8:** Work even on 7 sc.
- **Row 9 (toes):** Sc in first sc, * ch 5, sc in next 2 sc, repeat from *, end with sc in last 2 sc.
- End yarn and work ends in.

Ears/Flippers
Make 2.
- Work rows 1–5 of "Feet."
- End yarn, leaving a 10 in. (25cm) tail for assembly.

Safety Note

Use safety eyes or embroider the features if the toy is intended for children or pets, as buttons could pose a choking hazard.

Finishing

- Using tapestry needle threaded with yarn ends, sew parts to body, using photographs as a guide.
- Attach feet to center bottom, ears to top of head, and flippers to side of body.
- Using embroidery needle and floss, embroider faces using diagrams as a guide. Or make crochet chains and attach for facial features.

Creative Options

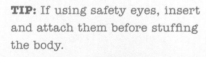

✳ The sky's the limit! Make your critter any way you like. Give him five eyes and three flippers if you want.

✳ Choose different types of yarn, such as furry and hairy yarns, to make a really unique critter.

✳ Try using different embellishments, such as tassels, feathers, buttons, trims, fringe, sequins, and glitter.

Felted Oven Mitts

These mitts aren't just handsome; they are also useful in the kitchen. Felted for durability and to handle the heat, the wool is moisture resistant as well. Make a set for yourself and gifts for your tasteful friends.

Finished Size:
Pre-felting: about 9 x 14 in. (23 x 36cm)
Post-felting: about 6 x 12 in. (15 x 30cm)

Techniques and Skills Used:
Chain stitch *(p. 17)*, **slip stitch** *(p. 18)*, **half-double crochet** *(p. 19)*

Note: The mitts are worked in the round with decreases and picking up stitches to shape. The completed item is felted to finish.

Finishing:
None required

Materials:
- **Yarn:** 100% wool worsted-weight yarn, shaded or variegated colors, 143 yd. (131m) per skein, 3 skeins
- **Crochet hook:** size J (5.5mm) or size needed for gauge
- **Novelty button trim:** 6 buttons (optional—see safety note)
- **Sewing needle and matching thread**
- **Tapestry or yarn needle**
- **Tape measure**
- **Scissors**

Pre-felting: 20 hdc/5½ in. (14cm) and 12 rows/4½ in. (11cm)
Post-felting: 20 hdc/4½ in. (11cm) and 12 rows/4 in. (10cm)

Note: Gauge is not critical, and it won't be exact after felting. Just be sure your after-felting measurements are close; a larger measurement is better than a smaller measurement.

Pattern Stitch:
The pattern stitch is simply half-double crochet.
- Ch 21.
- **Row 1:** Hdc in 3rd ch from hook and in each ch to end, ch 2 turn (20 hdc including beginning ch).
- **Row 2:** Skip 1st hdc, hdc in each stitch across, ch 2 turn.
- Repeat row 2 for 12 rows total.
Swatch measures 5½ in. x 4½ in. (14 x 11cm) before felting.

YARN AND SUBSTITUTION INFORMATION:

The yarn chosen for this project is a worsted-weight, 100% wool yarn. Yarn label information suggests 16 stitches to 4 in. (10cm) on size 8 (5mm) needles and 12 sc to 4 in. (10cm) with a size H (5mm) crochet hook.

Choose wool that has not been treated to be washable. Other yarns will not felt properly, so be sure to select one that will felt; avoid yarns labeled "superwash."

OVEN MITT
- Ch 59.
- **Row 1:** Hdc in 3rd ch from hook and in each ch to end, join to beginning ch 2, being careful not to twist work (58 hdc).
- **Round 1:** Ch 2, hdc in each stitch around, join with slip stitch in beginning ch 2.
- Continue to work in rounds until work measures 6 in. (15cm) from beginning.

Make Thumb Opening
- Skip next 14 hdc, continue hdc in rounds on 44 stitches.
- Work in rounds until piece measures 12 in. (30cm) from beginning.

Shape Top with Decrease Rounds
- **Decrease round:** Ch 2, * work 2 hdc together (decrease made), 10 hdc, repeat from * around, end 5 hdc, join with slip stitch to beginning ch 2 (40 hdc, including beginning ch 2).
- Work 1 round even.
- **Decrease round:** Ch 2, * work 2 hdc together (decrease made), 5 hdc, repeat from * around, end 2 hdc, join with slip stitch to beginning ch 2 (34 hdc, including beginning ch 2).
- Work one round even.
- **Decrease round:** Ch 2, * work 2 hdc together (decrease made), 1 hdc, repeat from * around, join with sl st to beginning ch 2 (23 hdc, including beginning ch 2).
- Work one round even.

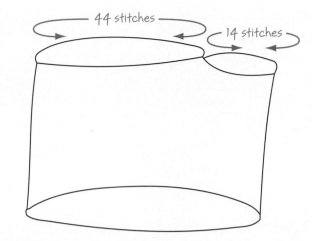

44 stitches 14 stitches

Safety Note

Use only heat-resistant trims on mitts for use in the kitchen.

- **Decrease round:** Ch 2, * work 2 hdc together (decrease made), 1 hdc, repeat from * around, end 2 hdc, join with slip stitch to beginning ch 2 (16 hdc, including beginning ch 2).
- End yarn, thread tail in tapestry needle, sew around opening and draw up to close. Work ends in.
- Make matching mitt.

Felting

- Felt (p. 28).

Finishing

- With sewing needle and matching thread, sew buttons to front of mitts.

Creative Options

* Make stripes by carrying the unused color along the inside of the mitt. It will felt into the fabric when finished.

* Use wool in a contrasting color to embroider around the mitt cuffs after felting.

* Make the thumb a contrasting color and accent the cuffs with that color.

* Use up all your scraps of wool in random stripes. Work over the ends as you go for easier finishing.

Felted Hook Book

Make a book for yourself, or make personal gifts for your handy friends. This project also makes a great organizer for sewing notions and other stitching supplies. There's plenty of room inside for your essentials.

Finished Size:
Pre-felting: 8½ x 25 in. (22 x 63cm) for case and 3½ x 9 in. (9 x 23cm) for dividers
Post-felting: 6 x 6 in. (15 x 15cm) folded; about 6 x 19 in. (15 x 48cm) unfolded

Techniques and Skills Used:
Chain stitch *(p. 17)*, **half-double crochet** *(p. 19)*

Project Gauge:
Pre-felting: 20 hdc/ 5½ in. (14cm)
Post-felting: 20 hdc/ 4½ in. (11cm)

Note: Gauge is not critical, and it won't be exact after felting. Just be sure your post-felting measurements are close so the case isn't too small for the hooks.

Materials:
- **Yarn:** 100%, wool worsted-weight yarn, shaded or variegated colors, 143 yd. (131m) per skein, 3 skeins
- **Crochet hook:** size J (5.5mm) or size needed for gauge
- **1 large button**
- **Sewing needle and matching thread**
- **Tapestry or yarn needle**
- **Tape measure**
- **Scissors**

Finishing:
Felting *(p. 28)*, **assembly, attaching closure and tassel**

Note: The book and dividers are worked flat with no shaping. The completed parts are felted and then assembled with closures and embellishments attached.

Pattern Stitch:
The pattern stitch is half-double crochet.
- Ch 21.
- **Row 1:** Hdc in 3rd ch from hook and in each ch to end, ch 2, turn (20 hdc, including beginning ch 2).
- **Row 2:** Skip 1st hdc, hdc in each stitch across, ch 2, turn.
- Repeat row 2 for 12 rows total. Swatch measures 5½ in. (14cm) before felting and 4½ in. (11cm) after felting.

YARN AND SUBSTITUTION INFORMATION

The yarn chosen for this project is a worsted-weight, 100% wool yarn. Yarn label information suggests 16 stitches to 4 in. (10cm) on size 8 (5mm) needles and 12 sc to 4 in. (10cm) with a size H (5mm) crochet hook.

Choose wool that has not been treated to be washable. Other yarns will not felt properly, so be sure to select one that will felt. Do not use yarns labeled "superwash."

HOOK BOOK
Make Outer Case
- Ch 33.
- **Row 1:** Hdc in 3rd ch from hook and in each ch to end, ch 2 turn (32 hdc).
- **Row 2:** Skip 1st hdc, hdc in each stitch across, ch 2 turn.
- Repeat row 2 for 60 rows total or until piece measures 25 in. (63cm).
- Cut yarn and work ends in.

Make Dividers
- Ch 15.
- Work as for case until divider measures 9 in. (23cm).
- Cut yarn and work ends in.
- Make two.

Felting
- Felt (p. 28).

Finishing

- Using yarn and tapestry needle, sew dividers to ends. Trim divider to length if necessary after attaching.
- Using your hooks or other tools as a guide, stitch lines along divider to create pockets.
- Fold book into thirds to close.
- With matching yarn, chain approximately 8 in. (20cm) and end off. Attach chain to back of book approximately 1 in. (2.5cm) from center of folded edge.
- Attach button to front flap at center approximately 1 in. (2.5cm) from free edge.
- Make a 3 in. (7.6cm) tassel and attach to end of chain.
- Wrap chain around button to close.

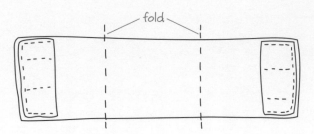

Assembly Diagram

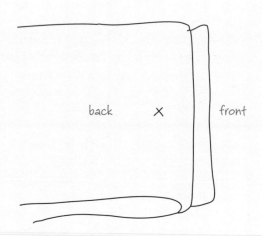

Closure

Creative Options

* Make a striped book—work two rows of one color and then one of another color, or make up your own scheme.

* Use up any leftover yarn in a random pattern. Just be sure all the yarns will felt.

* Customize your book with trims and appliqués from the notions aisle in your local craft store.

Care of Finished Projects

A handmade item deserves proper care to keep it looking good. Use these guidelines and your own common sense, and your projects will be fine.

Washing

Always save the label from the yarn because it will tell you how to launder the finished item. First, read the care instructions on the yarn label. Make sure that buttons and trims are secure and can be washed. Double-check the restrictions on buttons and trims. Some cannot be laundered, and others cannot be dry-cleaned. Remove them if necessary. Put the item in a laundry bag or pillowcase to protect it.

Wool, Blends, and Hand-Wash Only Items

Most care labels for wool, blends, and other animal fibers generally specify hand wash, and sometimes dry-cleaning, as the methods of care. To hand-wash your precious

woolens and delicates, you don't have to labor over a tub—use the washing machine to wash and rinse the sweater and spin the water out. Don't let the machine agitate the item or pour the water directly on it, however. Remember our felting lessons: felting is the result of mechanical agitation, heat, and sudden temperature changes.

Start with a mild, non-detergent soap. There are quite a few alternatives on the market now for washing woolens and other delicate items. Set the machine for the smallest load and use the delicate cycle. Run warm (not hot) water into the tub and add the soap while it runs. Don't use too much soap, or it could be difficult to rinse the item well. When the water has run in and the machine starts to agitate, turn it off.

Gently place your item into the water and carefully squeeze the soapy water through. Do this several times. Set the machine to spin and spin the water out of the tub. Be sure to stay close, as you need to be there for the rinse.

Stop the machine again at the end of the spin cycle and check that the item is not directly under the water spout. Be sure to check that the rinse water is the same temperature as the wash water. As before, gently squeeze the rinse water through the item and spin again.

Now that your project is clean and still damp, roll it in a towel and squeeze to remove as much

water as you can. If you have used the washing machine to spin the water out, there should not be a lot to remove. Find a moisture-resistant area large enough to hold the flat item. Drying screens are great. Dry smaller items on top of the dryer. Turn items frequently to dry both sides.

Hand-washing without the machine is the same as above, except you have to remove the water that the machine does in the spin cycle. Squeeze the water out—do not wring the item.

Some labels will say dry-clean only (specialty yarns may carry this label). Take the care method into consideration before investing the time to make the item. Some dry-clean-only yarns can be hand washed, but always test-wash a swatch before proceeding.

Cotton, Linen, and Similar Fibers

Items made from these fibers can often withstand hotter water and machine washing. However, drying them in the dryer usually results in a crumpled, misshapen item. Press them while slightly damp and let dry completely.

Pressing

Ironing and pressing are not recommended for items made of wool, blends, and synthetics, but 100% cotton responds beautifully to pressing. Press textured items on the wrong side on a thick towel to avoid flattening the stitches. A little spray starch adds crispness as well.

Storage

Before storing any handmade object, be sure it is clean. When your items are thoroughly dry, store them carefully. Moths like dark, damp conditions as well as soiled items. Silverfish can also damage cottons and linens when starched or stained items are left in storage. Keep your storage area dry, and air it and the stored garments occasionally.

When storing handmade items, moth and insect repellants are a good idea. These repellants range from old-fashioned mothballs to aromatic herbal materials. Be sure whatever you use does not come in contact with fabric. Plant materials that work well as insect repellants include rosemary, mint, thyme, cloves, cedar shavings, lavender, and other highly scented plants. You can even use a strong, fragrant bar of soap. Inspect and refresh any repellants and aromatics frequently.

Resources

Here is a collection of useful, and sometimes just plain cool, books and Web sites for knitting and crochet.

Web sites

craftster.org
An online forum for all types of craft and handwork—the place to ask specific questions

crochet.org
The Crochet Guild of America Web site dedicated to preserving and advancing the art of crochet

crochetinsider.com
Webzine to find news about developments in the industry, exchange ideas, and read designer interviews

crochetme.com
An online magazine for contemporary, cool, hip, and fashionable crochet

patternworks.com
A real treat in the mailbox—this catalog bills itself as "Everything for the hand knitter and crocheter"

shinydesigns.com
Information and patterns for knitting, crochet, and other types of needlework

yarndex.com
Great resource for finding information on specific yarns, such as weight, yardage, price, colors available, and even user reviews

yarnstandards.com
Sponsored by the Craft Yarn Council of America—standard guidelines on yarn weights, pattern difficulty levels, pattern sizing, and more

Books

The Crochet Answer Book: Solutions to Every Problem You'll Ever Face; Answers to Every Question You'll Ever Ask
By Edie Eckman
The title says it all

Couture Crochet Workshop; Mastering Fit, Fashion and Finesse
By Lily Chin
Technique information for creating finely finished crochet garments

The Harmony Guides: Basic Crochet Stitches, and *The Harmony Guides: Crochet Stitch Motifs*
Erika Knight, Ed.
Updated versions of the classic stitch dictionaries—excellent references

The "I Hate to Finish Sweaters" Guide to Finishing Sweaters
by Janet Szabo
A comprehensive guide to all aspects of finishing

The New Crochet: 40 Wonderful Wearables
by Terry Taylor
Stylish, contemporary patterns from a variety of artists that use familiar stitches

Stitch Collection; Textured Crochet
By Helen Jordan
A small dictionary with unusual and hard-to-find textured stitch patterns and motifs

ACKNOWLEDGMENTS

While writing this book, I learned even more just how much help other people have given me. Writing a book is a solitary task that, at the same time, requires tremendous assistance from others. I can't fully express how much I appreciate each person who has been involved, but my thanks go to all who have helped me in any way. Here are some who must be specially thanked.

My husband, a loving and patient man. Thank you for the many gifts you've given me.

My editor and friend, Karin Buckingham, a wonderful and creative woman. I consider myself lucky to have her guidance.

Everyone at Kalmbach Books, who take care of a thousand and more things to make a lovely finished book. A special thank you to Erica Swanson for many of the finishing details.

Mim Holden, who has worked with me on past books and stepped up again to make the projects for this book as well. Mim is incredibly talented, and I am so fortunate that she shares that talent with me.

Carolyn Hawkins, a sounding board and reality check for many of my ideas. She has shared much with me, from her time to her own unlimited creativity.

My mother, for her interest in my work and for helping me learn to crochet all those years ago.

Denise Miller and Melissa Chambers, for making a test critter or two.

The yarn companies who graciously and generously provided the yarns used in some of the projects: Cascade Yarns, Classic Elite Yarn Company, Malabrigo Yarns, and Lion Brand Yarn Company. Their contributions and assistance have helped tremendously in making the projects successful.

ABOUT THE AUTHOR

Monette Satterfield is an artist and freelance designer for the arts and crafts industry. She learned to embroider and crochet as a young girl. Learning to knit came later, but she took to it with great enthusiasm as well. Monette is a native of Florida, where heavy sweaters aren't worn much, but she still takes great pleasure in designing fashionable knit and crochet projects. She is also the author of *Knit & Crochet Combined: Best of Both Worlds* and *Let's Knit!*, both published by Kalmbach Books. You can visit her Web site at shinydesigns.com.

Create stylish accessories with expert how-to from **Let's Knit!**

Through 20 simple yet stylish projects, you'll learn knitting basics and the techniques that will help you build upon these skills. Work your needles with confidence to create garments, accessories, home items, and fun extras. Detailed stitch diagrams and an overview of materials and tools complete this handy resource.

62717 • $19.95

The **beginner's guide** to knitting

Let's Knit!

by Monette Satterfield

Learn fast with essential techniques, PLUS **20** step-by-step **projects**

Order online at www.KalmbachBooks.com or call **1-800-533-6644**

Monday-Friday, 8:30 a.m.-5:00 p.m. Central Time. Outside the U.S. and Canada, call 262-796-8776 x661.

KALMBACH BOOKS

PMK-BKS-62725RH